William W. Newton

A Father's Blessing

and other sermons for children

William W. Newton

A Father's Blessing
and other sermons for children

ISBN/EAN: 9783337266660

Printed in Europe, USA, Canada, Australia, Japan

Cover: Foto ©Lupo / pixelio.de

More available books at **www.hansebooks.com**

"A FATHER'S BLESSING."

THE PILGRIM SERIES.

BY THE REV. WM. W. NEWTON.

5 Vols. 16mo in a box, . . . $6.00.

CONTAINING

- I. LITTLE AND WISE $1.25
- II. THE WICKET-GATE 1.25
- III. THE INTERPRETER'S HOUSE. 1.25
- IV. THE PALACE BEAUTIFUL . . 1.25
- V. GREAT HEART. 1.25

"The lessons of wisdom are so charmingly interwoven with captivating little stories that while the interest of the young reader never flags, the good seed is unconsciously received into the child heart. There is no temptation to 'skip the stupid part,' for it is scarcely possible to say where the story ends and the sermonizing begins."—PEOPLE AND PULPIT.

BY DR. RICHARD NEWTON.

THE JEWEL CASE. 6 vols. . . . $7.50

THE BEST THINGS	$1.25	BIBLE BLESSINGS	$1.25
THE KING'S HIGHWAY . .	1.25	THE GREAT PILOT	1.25
THE SAFE COMPASS. . . .	1.25	BIBLE JEWELS	1.25

THE WONDER CASE. 6 vols. . . $7.50

BIBLE WONDERS.	$1.25	THE JEWISH TABERNACLE .	$1.25
NATURE'S WONDERS . . .	1.25	RILLS FROM THE FOUNTAINS.	1.25
LEAVES FROM TREE OF LIFE.	1.25	GIANTS, AND WONDERS . .	1.25

- RAYS FROM THE SUN OF RIGHTEOUSNESS $1.25
- THE KING IN HIS BEAUTY. 1.25
- PEBBLES FROM THE BROOK. 1.25
- BIBLE PROMISES. 1.25
- BIBLE WARNINGS 1.25

ROBERT CARTER & BROTHERS,
NEW YORK.

"A FATHER'S BLESSING"

AND

Other Sermons for Children

BY

WILLIAM WILBERFORCE NEWTON

AUTHOR OF "LITTLE AND WISE," "THE WICKET-GATE," "INTERPRETER'S HOUSE," "PALACE BEAUTIFUL," "GREAT HEART"

"Bless me, even me also, O my Father!"

NEW YORK
ROBERT CARTER AND BROTHERS
530 BROADWAY

COPYRIGHT, 1888,
BY ROBERT CARTER & BROTHERS.

ELECTROTYPED BY
THE ORPHANS' PRESS—CHURCH CHARITY FOUNDATION, BROOKLYN.
CAMBRIDGE PRESS—JOHN WILSON & SONS.

PREFACE.

Some time ago my dear Father asked me what he should take up as his next course of sermons to children. I suggested as a good subject the blessing of Jacob upon his twelve sons. His reply was, "I don't think that is in my line: you write a course on that subject, and I will take up a course on Bible animals." When I came to write the last sermon in this course, he had finished one half of the sermons laid out in his plan, and lay dying at his home at Chestnut Hill, Philadelphia.

As I go on with the work he has left, and complete his unfinished course, I take a sad satisfaction in bidding his little friends and readers farewell, in this last book of sermons which, strangely enough, was named long before he died:

"A FATHER'S BLESSING."

PITTSFIELD, MASS.
Jan. 1, 1888.

CONTENTS.

CHAPTER	PAGE
1. The Blessing of Reuben, the Unstable Son.	9
2. Simeon and Levi, the Cruel Sons.	25
3. Judah, the Successful Son	41
4. Zebulon, the Sailor Son.	55
5. Issachar, the Unambitious Son.	69
6. Dan, the Deceitful Son	85
7. Gad, the Persevering Son	101
8. Asher, the Self-Indulgent Son	117
9. Naphtali, the Light-minded Son	131
10. Joseph, the Fruitful Son	141
11. Benjamin, the Son of the Right Hand.	155
12. The Father himself, who Blessed his Boys.	169
13. Realized Dreams	181
14. Lessons from the Clock.	195

CHAPTER	PAGE
15. Dogs.	211
16. The Power of a Fact.	225
17. Satan's Fishing Tackle	243
18. The Man who Saved, and the Man who Taxed.	257
19. School-boy Saints	269
20. Wells and Water Pipes.	283
21. Innocency	293
22. Lessons from the Ferry Boat.	309
23. "Spirits in Prison"	321
24. "The Lion and the Bear".	333

I.

THE BLESSING OF REUBEN; or, THE UNSTABLE SON.

"Unstable as water, thou shalt not excel."
GENESIS xlix. 4.

YOU all know the story of Jacob and Esau, and how the younger supplanted his older brother, and stole his father Isaac's blessing. And you remember, too, how that stolen blessing proved a curse, until the robber son made atonement for the gift which he had stolen.

Now I am going to speak to you in this course of children's sermons, about

"A FATHER'S BLESSING."

The old man in the story is the dying Jacob—the same who in his youth had robbed his brother of his birthright. He is now at the end of his long and troubled life. His face is turned to the wall and his children are kneeling around his bedside. Most of his sons had been hard and wicked boys. They had given their father no end of sorrow and trouble, and had brought down his gray hair with sorrow to the grave. But now the past was all over; the aged patriarch had only a few more hours to live, and before he died he wanted to give to each of his children the blessing or the judgment which their life deserved. "And Jacob called unto his sons and said, 'Gather yourselves together that I may tell you that which shall befall you in the last days. Gather yourselves and hear, ye sons of Jacob, and hearken unto Israel, your father.'"

The first blessing which the dying old man uttered was upon his oldest son, Reuben.

"Reuben," he said, "thou art my first born, my might and the beginning of my strength, the excellency of dignity and the excellency of power. Unstable as water, thou shalt not excel."

Reuben was the unstable son of the family. He was the oldest and ought to have set a good example. As it was he was weak and infirm of purpose. So then there was not much of a blessing upon this irresolute and wayward son. Instability had been his curse and temptation. His life was a failure because of his unstable character. And I suppose it was because of this instability of Reuben's nature, which was a fault his father had long before found out in him, that Jacob refused to let Benjamin go with him down to Egypt, when the long-lost Joseph sent for him. "And Reuben spake unto his father, saying: Slay my two sons if I bring him not to thee: deliver him into my hand and I will bring him to thee again.

"And he said, My son shall not go down with you: for his brother is dead and he is left alone: if mischief befall him in the way in which you go, then shall ye bring down my gray hairs with sorrow to the grave" (Gen. xlii. 26). If Jacob had trusted Reuben, he would undoubtedly have let Benjamin go with him.

Instability is a great fault in our character, and surely brings a curse upon us. It ruins us if we become unstable ourselves, or get the reputation of instability fastened upon us.

A large party of gentlemen some time ago went camping out in the Adirondack woods. They had guides and boats and dogs and tents in great abundance.

There was a famous doctor in the party, who was a great shot, and always brought home at night the game he started out to find.

One day he took one of the small boys in the party along with him. The boy's name was Jack. Jack wanted to stop and shoot at every stump and small bird on their trail.

Presently he saw a great number of swallows skimming along the lake.

"Doctor, doctor! There are plenty of birds," called out Jack. "Why don't you fire?"

"Because," said the doctor, "I've come out

for ducks; and when I go for ducks, I never stop to shoot at small birds."

Now, my dear children, the trouble with many of us in life is just this. We stop to hunt for trifles when we ought to be going for larger results. If we go for ducks, we ought not to stop for mere swallows; for if we stop to catch every little thing in our way, we never will bring home any large returns of our labor.

You have all read about the yacht race of the American boat, the Puritan, with the Genesta, the English yacht which came over here to take away the prize cup.

Now, suppose that the captain of the Puritan had altered his course on that exciting race, every time some friend thought he could make a better run in some different way; or suppose he had stopped a while to catch a school of blue fish, which had come in his path, where would have been his prize at the end of the race?

No huntsman can excel in a day's shooting if he stops for every little trifle. No captain can drive his boat on the winning side who stops or bends his course at the advice of every friend.

To be successful in every department of life, we must keep to our course, and not turn aside for the sake of trifles.

An unstable, irresolute, uncertain nature never, never can win in the race of life.

There are three reasons why instability of character makes us like this son Reuben, and keeps one from excelling.

I.

The first reason is:

Because an unstable person has no standard of living. Everything that has life in it must have some standard or scale of action.

A carrier pigeon which flies hundreds of miles from city to city over rivers and mountains, travels at a regular and uniform rate of speed. The wild ducks which fly south along the Atlantic seaboard in October, fly at a regular rate of about eighty miles an hour.

There is no instability about the carrier pigeons or the wild ducks. They know the point they are going to, and never bend their course to suit any mere whim of the moment.

Here are two clocks. They are each wound up, and ought to go correctly. One of them does go, in as even and regular a way as it can, and tries to keep as near to the sun's time as it is possible to do. The other goes for a while, and then stops; and afterwards, when it tumbles down, or when somebody knocks it, goes on again.

Which of these clocks would you trust? Which of them would you want to have as your standard of time by which to regulate your engagements? Certainly you would not want the Reuben-like clock, the unstable and uncertain time-piece. If we do not know what the true time is, we will miss the train, and lose the steamboat, and be late to school and to church, and will have everything go wrong with us, and be behind time continually.

An unstable clock is a poor thing to run one's life by. We are never sure of the hour, and can never be punctual and exact in meeting our duties.

And an unstable character is just like an unstable clock. Sometimes the unstable person is before time and sometimes he is behind time. Sometimes he is full of zeal, and sometimes he is dull and tedious. At one time we can depend upon him—at another time he is not to be counted on at all. To-day he is glad to see us; to-morrow he passes us by without a word.

An unstable person is a poor companion; a poor friend; a poor worker.

No matter what powers or gifts or graces of character any of us may have, if we are unstable and uncertain and cannot be depended upon, we are poor, worthless things. Pray God, my dear children, to help you get the better over this terrible fault, for if it grows upon you it will turn all your life blessings into a curse, as it did with this poor Reuben, Jacob's oldest son. Instability of character keeps us from excelling in the first place, because an unstable person has no standard of living.

II.

Secondly.—Instability of character keeps us from excelling, because an unstable person can never be trusted.

If we were going to sail for Europe to-morrow in one of the great ocean steamers, we should want to be sure that the vessel would sail in a direct course for the haven where we would be. Suppose a steamer should take upon itself in mid ocean to stop for a week, or to start up and go to Greenland or Brazil, regardless of the compass or the will of the man at the wheel, we would certainly be in a very bad fix. We should not know where we were, or whither we were going! But being on board an unstable steamer is about the same thing as being bound to an unstable friend or adviser.

Sometimes strong and steady parents have weak and irresolute children; and sometimes it is the children who have unstable and uncertain parents. But in either case, the unstable members of a family can never be trusted. They "forgot," and they "didn't think," and they were carried away by the mere thought of the moment, and never once thought of their duty; and after trying these unstable people over and over again, after a while we learn to put no trust in them.

I suppose the old patriarch Jacob had tried his boy Reuben very many times, and had found out that he could never be trusted, so that he would not think for one moment of letting him take charge of his son Benjamin, when he wanted to take him down to see his brother Joseph in Egypt.

Some years ago a family from the east moved out to the far west and began to clear the ground in order to have a farm. There was a boy in the family named Tom, who used to help his father on the farm in many ways. But he was an uncertain kind of boy, and never could be found when he was wanted.

One day his father and the men on the farm were moving logs. Tom was helping them in his way. His work was to pick up the rollers and put them under the logs, while his father and the men were bearing down on the other end of the log.

"Now, Tom," cried his father, as they all pressed down on their end of the log, "now be quick there, and slide the roller under the other end of the log."

"Yes, sir, yes, sir," called out Tom, "I'll be there in a minute. I saw a woodchuck, just now, and I'm going off to catch it."

So the farm hands had to do Tom's work for him, and got into the way of never counting upon Tom any more.

Some years after this, a friend of the family was passing by the house, and asked the man who was driving him what had become of the different members of the family.

The driver told the stranger the story about the boy Tom and the woodchuck, and then added, "and now the old judge, Tom's father, is dead, and Tom's a grown-up man, but stranger, he's been catching woodchucks ever since he was a boy, and he'll go on catching woodchucks all the way to the end of his life."

Dear children, do not let us be mere woodchuck hunters through this life of ours. Do not let us spend our time in an uncertain and irresolute kind of life, throwing away our days over the mere accidents and trifles of life. The habit of catching *woodchucks* when we ought to be *moving logs*, will grow upon us if we do not keep it down.

And if we become unstable, irresolute characters, running after trifles when we ought to be doing our steady, solid work, people will leave us to ourselves, because they will feel that we never can be trusted.

III.

Thirdly and Lastly.—Instability of character keeps us from excelling, because an unstable person has no power of endurance. The quality of endurance is a strong and conquering power. Sometimes we want strength to accomplish certain things. At other times we want strength to endure. The strength of endurance is at times a greater blessing than the strength of accomplishing things.

St. Paul says, in his Epistle to Timothy, "This one thing I do," as if he did this one thing at a time to keep himself from the great temptation of trying to do too many things.

At a certain point in the battle of Waterloo, before it was at all clear that victory was coming to the English, the Duke of Wellington was greatly annoyed by a certain general who sent word to him to know what he should do.

"Stand firm," replied the Duke.

Presently another courier rode up to the side of the English commander with a second message from the division general. "We are being shot to pieces," wrote the general. "What shall we do?"

The Duke took out a card and wrote on it the words "Stand firm."

Half an hour afterwards a third courier came galloping up to the Duke.

He brought still another message to the English leader. The message was this: "The enemy are turning our flank, and are pouring bullets into our side. What shall we do?"

The Iron Duke wrote on a scrap of paper his third message, "*Stand firm.*"

After this the General sent no more messages to the Duke, for he knew beforehand what the orders would be. And it was because this division stood firm and wore out the attacks by Napoleon, that the English were enabled a little while later to reap the great victory of Waterloo. But if the Duke of Wellington had been a Reuben, he never would have been victorious, for of all the Reubens in the world the words of the old dying Jacob are true, "Unstable as water thou shalt not excel."

There was a minister once who was ordained with high hopes of success. Every one predicted that he would have great success, and be a very useful minister. But he had one hidden defect, which did not come out in life until the hard experiences of life brought it out.

He was a Reuben. He was an unstable son, but he did not know it.

He gave up the first parish he had because they had limewater there. Then he gave up his second church because they had bad butter in the place. His third parish did not suit him because of the salt air; and he couldn't get on in his fourth parish because of a certain Captain Crooks who was warden in it. At last, after moving about twelve or thirteen times, and wearing his poor wife and family out, he found that there was bad butter, or limestone water, or bad air, or a Captain Crooks in every parish, and that the trouble was not with his surroundings, but was with his own poor, weak, miserable, unstable self.

He was a Reuben. He was an unstable son, and because of this great defect in his life, the prophecy of Jacob was fulfilled in his case—"Unstable as water thou shalt not excel."

Now, my dear children, remember the lessons of this sermon to-day upon Reuben, the unstable son.

Instability keeps us from excelling.

Firstly.—Because an unstable person has no standard of living.

Secondly.—Because an unstable person can never be trusted.

Thirdly.—Because an unstable person has no power of endurance.

Remember this sermon on poor Reuben. His father could not say very much that was good about him when he came to die. So his blessing was changed into a judgment and stands on the page of Scripture as a Bible warning against

"The Unstable Son."

II.

SIMEON AND LEVI; or, THE CRUEL SONS.

"Simeon and Levi are brethren; instruments of cruelty are in their habitations. O my soul, come not thou into their secret: unto their assembly, mine honor, be not thou united; for in their anger they slew a man, and in their self-will they digged down a wall. Cursed be their anger, for it was fierce; and their wrath, for it was cruel: I will divide them in Jacob, and scatter them in Israel."—GENESIS xlix. 5, 6, 7.

IT is a terrible moment to us when we are sitting in a dentist's chair waiting for him to find the right instrument with which to take out our aching tooth. If the tooth were not so cruel, it would not drive us to that dreadful place. If the dentist's instruments were not so cruel, we would not mind sitting there. But it is the choice of evils which troubles us so much. While the tooth is throbbing away with its nerves and roots (its instruments of cruelty), the dentist stands before his cabinet debating with himself which of all his many instruments of cruelty will best do the work for us. And thus it comes to pass that we are in a bad plight either way; for whichever way we turn, we see Simeon and Levi about us, with instruments of cruelty in their hands.

Cruelty is a remnant of the beast-nature within us. If we were left to ourselves, without any moral or religious restraint or guidance, we would become as cruel as the beasts about us.

We cannot read the pages of history without seeing at every turn the signs of human nature's cruelty. Think of the way in which people in the name of God and for the sake of what they called "the truth," persecuted their fellow-men. Fox's Book of Martyrs is a book which we all love to read when we are young. It is filled with stories and pictures of the most terrible persecutions that it is possible to imagine. When I was a little boy I used to read this book on Sunday afternoons, after a comfortable Sunday dinner, and used to feel very thankful that I did not live in that far-off Simeon and Levi age.

Animals are cruel by nature. There is an old hymn, by Isaac Watts, in the nursery primers, which begins in this way:

> "Let dogs delight to bark and bite,
>   For 'tis their nature to;
> Let bears and lions growl and fight,
>   For God hath made them so."

How the tiger teases its prey! How the cat plays with the poor, frightened little mouse before she kills it! How the spider seems to gloat over the fly which it has caught in its web! "Instruments of cruelty" are plainly visible at every turn in the animal world. The shark's tooth, the lobster's claw, the bull's horns, the cat's claws, are the weapons of warfare by which the animal creation make war on one another and defend themselves.

But the beast nature has nothing to do

with the kingdom of Heaven, and can never enter it.

And whatever we have of the beast nature must be thrown off before we can be where our Lord Jesus Christ and the blessed saints are.

Simeon and Levi were cruel sons. We do not know much about them, but what we do know is bad. The old patriarch Jacob could not find anything good to say about these hard-hearted boys of his, and so he turned his blessing into a judgment, and uttered these words of our text:

"Simeon and Levi are brethren; instruments of cruelty are in their habitations. O my soul, come not thou into their secret: unto their assembly, mine honor, be not thou united; for in their anger they slew a man, and in their self-will they digged down a wall. Cursed be their anger, for it was fierce; and their wrath, for it was cruel: I will divide them in Jacob, and scatter them in Israel."

There were four distinct things which the

dying Jacob mentioned about his cruel sons —Simeon and Levi. And the same four things are found to be connected with all cruel children.

I.

First of all:

Cruel children always seek for instruments of cruelty. It is hard to be cruel if we have nothing to be cruel with. But if we have a club, or a whip, or a pair of spurs, or a bowgun, then we will seek to find some animal to try our weapons on.

But it is hard work to be cruel if we have no instruments of cruelty. A nation that has got no standing army will not seek to go to war. But a country which is filled with soldiers will always be wanting to fight. Some time ago I was in a police court where a young man was being tried for a stabbing affray. He had tried to stab another young man, and when he could not succeed in doing this he fired a pistol after his enemy and wounded him in the leg.

The Judge asked the prisoner what induced him to carry such weapons as those. The boy replied that he had seen these daggers and pistols in the window of a cutlery shop, and that after looking at them in the shop window every night on his way home from work, he saved up his money and bought them ; and that when he had bought them, he was not happy until he had used them in some way.

Now, my dear children, depend upon it, instruments of cruelty around us educate us in the art of being cruel.

It would not have occurred to this boy to want to stab if he had not owned a dagger. We can save just one-half of the consequences of our sins by avoiding the temptations which lead to them. Many a murderer would have been saved his shameful death upon the gallows, if he had not had about his person, at the time of his anger, some weapon or instrument of death. Cruelty grows upon us before we know it. One of the noblest societies of our land is the great Society for the Prevention of Cruelty to Animals. This society can arrest angry teamsters for beating their horses unmercifully. It establishes fountains for the poor, thirsty horses to drink at, and in many ways takes away the instruments of cruelty out of the hands of those who do not know how to be kind to dumb animals.

One of the first blessings which Jesus uttered in his Sermon on the Mount, is the blessing on the merciful. "Blessed are the merciful," he said," for they shall obtain mercy." Implements of kindness teach us to be kind: but instruments of cruelty will make us as they made Simeon and Levi — hardhearted, cruel sons.

II.

Secondly.—Cruel children always go together into cruelty.

It is a very singular thing how children always love to have "secrets." Sometimes these secrets are good, and sometimes they are bad. Sometimes they lead the way to a pleasant surprise, as the secret of a birthday present, or the secrets of Christmas time; and at other times they lead the way to mischief and sorrow.

Now it is very evident that Simeon and Levi had got, at a certain period in their life, into some great trouble. They had some plot or intrigue, some scheme of mischief or secret conspiracy which they kept to themselves, and out of this plot there grew a quarrel, and the result of it all was that they killed a man and digged down some stone wall over which they had been struggling.

There is an old saying that it takes two to make a quarrel. It is very difficult for a person to have a secret plot or conspiracy all to one's self. When we go into mischief and cruelty, we always go in company. It is very hard to be cruel without some instrument of cruelty in our hands, and without some companions, to share the blame of sin with us.

Cruel people always have an instrument of cruelty, and some secret of cruelty, and some cruel companions to help bear them out in their wicked ways. This was the way it was with Simeon and Levi. And this is the way it has always been with cruel people in the world.

In the days of James the First of England, there was a plot among certain nobles to blow up the House of Parliament, and bring in new rulers of the kingdom. One of the principal characters in this conspiracy was a noble names Catesby. He wanted to blow up all the members of the House of Lords, with the exception of a certain friend of his named Lord Monteagle.

So he wrote Lord Monteagle a letter, telling him he had better keep away from the Houses of Parliament on a certain day. "For God and man," said Catesby in his letter, "have concurred to punish the wickedness of the times." This letter seemed so suspicious that Lord Monteagle showed it to some of his friends. They began to hunt about for suspicious-looking persons; and on going down into the cellar of the House of Lords, they discovered an evil-looking man, whose name was Guy Fawkes, about to light a slow match which communicated with a number of barrels of gunpowder. This plot was called the Gunpowder Plot. The 5th day of November, the day on which Guy Fawkes was discovered, was called "Guy Fawkes' day," and ever afterwards, the boys of England used to keep the day, as our boys keep the Fourth of July, by dressing up an image to look like Guy Fawkes. Then after marching about with him for a time, they would take him to a bonfire to be burned.

Now this famous gunpowder plot in English history, shows us what is meant by a conspiracy of cruel people—such as the plot which Simeon and Levi had. There was "a secret and an assembly," and "instruments of cruelty," and "anger," and "self-will," and companionship in this cruel plot.

My dear children, let me beg you not to have "secrets," or "instruments of cruelty," or companions, if these lead you into anger and self-will.

Remember the second lesson of our subject to-day. It is like the old proverb, "birds of a feather flock together." Do not forget this lesson. Cruel children always go together into mischief.

III.

Thirdly.—Cruel children are always governed by their passions.

The older we grow the more truly we find that our passions are fearful companions. We must keep them under control all the way through life. If they ever get the mastery over us, they will act like runaway horses and will dash us to pieces.

A furnace to an engine makes it go, so long as the fires are held under control. But the moment the fires cease to obey the engineer, that moment there is danger ahead.

The volcanic outburst, the hurricane at sea, the cyclone on land are the passions of nature, and are pictures of the passions within us. What a description of our evil nature is this verse of our text to-day. " Cursed be heir anger for it was fierce, and their wrath for it was cruel. I will divide them in Jacob and scatter them in Israel." I suppose you have all read that old story of little Red Riding Hood. Well, you remember how the wolf, in the grandmother's clothes, disguised himself until the night-time came, in order to eat up little Red Riding Hood. He waited a long time for his prey, but at last the cruel wolf showed himself. And our fierce and cruel passions wait a long time until the right moment comes for them to bite and devour their prey. They may be disguised now, as a cat's claws are hidden under their velvety fur, when she purs under the stroking she receives, but when any sudden temptation comes, out will come the evil passions, as the cat's claws come out whenever a dog bounces into her presence.

There was once an old German father who tried to make something good and useful out of his boy. But the son was an artist, and liked to dream and paint and skip his day's work on the farm whenever he could do so.

At last, just before his son left him to go

to Paris, where he was about to study art, the old father said to him:—

"Tony, my son, remember this last advice of your old father. Our passions are our greatest enemies. What we want to do is to be able to command them. The discipline of the human will is the secret of durable conquests and long happiness. Tony, I have always loved the crowing of the cock. It announces the day, and chases away the phantoms of the night. The sound resembles a war-cry. It admonishes us to spend our lives in fighting against ourselves."

A year or two after this, when his father had died, Tony, now a rising young artist in Paris, was tempted by his companions to join a band of gamblers, who were making money at the expense of foreigners in Paris. One night, when he was lying awake, thinking over in his mind whether or not he should go with these bad companions, he heard a cock crow. Like the crowing of the cock which brought to Simon Peter's memory the words of Jesus, the sound of the crowing brought back to Tony the last words of his honest old father. That morning crow sounded to him like a voice from his father's grave, and it turned the scale of his will. He said no, to his tempters, and gained the victory over the evil passions within him.

Let us learn the great lesson of Jacob's judgment upon his cruel sons, that cruel children are those who instead of *ruling* their passions are *governed* by them.

IV.

The fourth and last lesson of our subject is, that cruel children are always left to themselves. Jacob said of Simeon and Levi, who could not control their cruel tempers:

"I will divide them in Jacob and scatter them in Israel." These sons of Jacob were not wanted by their brethren. The other sons would rather be alone than have these cruel fellows keep company with them, with their instruments of cruelty about them. Cruel children are always left alone. Boys who crowd, kick, pinch, tease and use their friends for pin cushions, into whom they can run twisted pins, are not agreeable companions.

Every now and then, as we walk through the streets of our cities, we see in the various store-windows the sign, "Boy wanted." But boys who keep instruments and habits of cruelty about them are never wanted. Nobody cares for the company of those cruel sons except Satan. But they are just what he wants. Satan is always after the Simeon and Levi kind of children.

As we grow older, my dear children, life becomes a very lonely thing. We grow away from our friends; and our friends die. Our parents are taken from us, and new people appear who do not care anything for us. We want above all things else to keep our friends, and not to lose them.

And there is no way by which we can keep our friends by our side so surely as by using kind words and doing kind deeds for them. But harsh words and unkind actions are never, never forgotten.

Remember then, I beg you, my dear children, these four lessons which we learn from the judgment of Jacob upon his cruel sons, Simeon and Levi.

Cruel children always seek for instruments of cruelty.

Cruel children always go together into mischief.

Cruel children are always governed by their passions; and

Cruel children are always left to themselves.

Poor old Jacob could not say anything good about these two cruel sons when he came to die. What will our friends say of us when we pass away? Will they utter a blessing over us for our kindness, or will they pronounce a judgment on us for our sins?

III.

THE BLESSING OF JUDAH; or, "THE SUCCESSFUL SON."

"Judah, thou art he whom thy brethren shall praise. Thy hand shall be in the neck of thine enemies. Thy father's children shall bow down to thee."—GENESIS xlix. 8.

A GREAT French wit once said, "Success always succeeds." We may say of course it does, but the wonderful thing about success is that we do not recognize it as such until it does succeed. There is something very singular about success. We cannot describe it. We cannot predict it. We cannot tell exactly in what it consists, but we can all see it and feel it. It is something which we can feel even if we cannot describe it.

Judah was the successful son in his father's family. Everything he did seemed to succeed. The tribe of Judah grew to be the most powerful of all the tribes, and finally stood for the entire Kingdom of Israel.

And it was because Jacob the father of this successful son Judah, saw by prophesy all his boy's future greatness, that he uttered these words of blessing over his head, "Judah, Thou art he whom thy brethren shall praise. Thy hand shall be in the neck of thine enemies. Thy father's children shall bow down before Thee. Judah is a lion's whelp; from the prey my son thou art gone up; he stooped down, he couched as a lion, and as an old lion: who shall rouse him up?"

There is a successful son in almost every family. Somehow or other he manages to succeed while the others fail and flounder about in their efforts. No one can tell just how this is, or just why it is, but the fact remains that it is so. Brothers and sisters may criticise and find fault with this Judah, but still he goes on succeeding every time, while the rest of them only talk about success and strive in every way to secure it.

In the family of Jacob, Judah's brethren may have said that it was all luck on his part, and that he was peculiarly fortunate in everything he accomplished. But the old patriarch Jacob knew better than this. He said that Judah would not be lucky but successful. He saw in his boy before him, the elements of that success which in after years would make him famous. And so the old man uttered this blessing upon his boy:

"Judah, Thou art he whom thy brethren shall praise. Thy hand shall be in the neck of thine enemies. Thy father's children shall bow down to thee."

I want to speak to you to-day in this sermon on "The Successful Son," about the difference between *luck* and *success*.

I.

First of all I would say—Luck waits for the opportunity to come to us; success goes and finds the opportunity.

For instance here is a colony of bees and a group of grasshoppers. It is summer time.

They are all alike, singing and buzzing in the meadow. The grasshoppers are lazy indolent fellows, while the bees are as busy as they can be. The grasshoppers take no care for the morrow; the bees on the other hand are laying up honey all the day for the winter's use in the hive. The grasshoppers wait for the honey to come to them, and the consequence is they will starve in the winter time. The bees go hard to work to find the honey, and the result of their labor is that they will be fed in the hive while their neighbors, the grasshoppers, will be dying of starvation. That is the difference between waiting for luck to come to one, and going out to find one's luck in honest labor.

There were two boys once, named Jack and Richard, whose father set aside a plot of ground for them to take care of. He promised them a reward, if their gardens looked well at the end of the season.

Jack used to go and look at his garden every little while, and resolve that by and by, when he saw anything to do in it he would do it. Richard, on the other hand, trimmed every plant and tree; weeded the beds, cleared off all the potato bugs, and never let the weeds get a single week's growth in advance of him. At the end of the summer their father took a walk with the boys in their gardens. "Why Jack," said the father, "you are no kind of a gardener, look at the weeds in your garden bed!"

"That's just what I always said," replied Jack, "Richard is always lucky in his gardening; besides his soil is richer than mine, and things grow in it better than they do with me."

"Nonsense," replied his father, "what you call Richard's luck is his honest toil, and what you call your poor soil is your own idleness. So Richard gets the Waterbury watch I promised to the best gardener." Now, my dear children, we must all be very careful how we confound our own stupidity with bad luck, and get into the way of calling the hard work of others their good luck.

Take for instance the man in our Lord's

parable of the talents, who hid his one talent in a napkin. The other servants in that parable did something with their talents. They went out of their narrow little life at home and accomplished something. They did not wish for a great find of good luck to come to them. But the man with one talent did nothing. He waited and waited for the opportunity to come to him, instead of going bravely to seek the opportunity. And the Lord in the parable called him a wicked and slothful servant, because he trusted to some sort of good luck coming to him, instead of going to find the opportunity of working. Remember this first lesson of our subject, the difference between luck and success. Luck waits for the opportunity to come to us; success goes and finds the opportunity.

II.

Secondly.—Luck is the weapon of the gambler; work is the weapon of the honest man.

We never want to be considered successful in any dishonest way. To deceive or to be selfish, or to be dishonest and thereby to gain an end, is not to be successful. Success which is gained at the expense of the right or by stamping one's conscience under foot is not success. But at the same time we want to remember that success is something which can be earned, and is not alone something to be waited for.

There are a great many people in the world who believe that they must wait until good luck comes to them. Now, my dear children, all such people are mere gamblers. They have no honest tools. All the instruments they have are dice and cards and tricks of hand. People who believe in luck, and wait for luck, and count upon luck, are, in spirit, gamblers. They are waiting for success to come to them.

The Judah-like people on the other hand are those who earn their own success. They do not believe that they are born under lucky or unlucky stars; or that they were or were not born with a silver spoon in their mouth. They work their way up to power by their own exertions. Now, my dear children, you will find out that there are two things which mark the successful people in the world.

First of all—the Judah-like men and women of the world pay careful attention to the little things of life. It is the little things of life which go to make up the great things. It is attention to the little details, which, without making us fussy or small-minded, will help to make us careful and thorough and systematic. And then secondly—the Judah-like men and women of the world who are successful are always marked by indomitable perseverance. The bull-dog is the strongest of all dogs, simply because when he gets a grip on another dog he never lets go until one or the other is dead. The other day I was looking at some prize bull-dogs which were worth five hundred dollars a piece. It seemed to me as if they must be tired of holding up their big jaws, they looked so heavy. But it was their big jaws which gave them their power over all the other dogs.

And the one thing which made Gen. Grant the Judah that he was among all the other generals of the war, was the fact that he held on amid all sorts of difficulties, and never was beaten, because he never knew when he was beaten. When he was a boy at school, it was said that he never walked back to the place that he started from, but always walked around the place until he got back again to the place from which he started out.

Attention to the little matters and bull dog perseverance are the two signs of the Judahs in the world. The Judah men do not trust to luck: they depend upon their own exertions in order to achieve success.

III.

Thirdly.—Luck finds fault with its own instruments; success never blames its own tools.

You know, it is said that it is the poor workman who blames his tools.

When the lucky man begins to be unlucky he instantly goes to work to curse his lot, and his surroundings, and his family. The successful man, on the other hand, does not blame his instruments; he looks into his own character to see if he cannot find the cause of all his trouble. There is an old song in Dr. Watts' Nursery Hymns which I shall never forget. It begins,

>"'Tis the voice of the sluggard,
> I heard him complain,
> You have waked me too soon,
> I must slumber again."

The sluggard finds fault with the clock. But the clock is all right. The sun is all right. The daylight is all right. The fault is with the sleepy man who does not want to get up. When I hear people going about complaining of their friends, and their relations, and the place where they live, and the kind of work they have to do, I always make up my mind that the trouble is with their own works, in their own characters, and not with the outside world. Depend upon it, my dear children, people who continually blame their tools have never had the blessing which came upon Judah descend upon them. Their fathers' children will never bow down to them, because they themselves have never bowed down to honest labor. They have bowed to pleasure, not to duty.

IV.

Fourthly and lastly.—I would say that luck is the spoiled child of Fortune; success is the child of honest toil.

A spoiled child grows after a while to be a great nuisance about the house. We can put up with it for a short time, but we soon grow tired of its waywardness and its whims.

We all need to be disciplined in order to bring forth any good results in our life and character.

If we do not learn to obey we can never be fit to command. If we do not learn to throw aside this idea of being lucky; if we keep waiting for Nature to be making us handsome presents all the time; if we get into the way of expecting a run of luck instead of doing honest work ourselves, we will wait in vain for true success to come to us. We must work: we must toil: we must be patient: we must be persevering if we would win true success in life. Success is a trained and dutiful child: it is born out of honest toil. Luck is the spoiled child of fortune, and can never be counted upon in any enterprise.

Remember, then, my dear children, these four lessons of our subject to-day.

I. Luck waits for the opportunity to come to us; success goes and finds the opportunity.

II. Luck is the weapon of the gambler; work is the weapon of the successful man.

III. Luck finds fault with its own instruments; success never blames its own tools.

IV. Luck is the spoiled child of Fortune; success is the child of honest toil.

"Judah, Thou art he whom thy brethren shall praise. Thy father's children shall bow down to thee."

This was the old man's blessing upon Judah, the successful son of the family.

His brethren may have said that he was lucky, but the old Jacob said that he was successful. And his success came to him not because he had a run of luck, but because he knew how to take hold of the problem of living. Children! do not crave luck, or fortune; *crave success, and see to it that you earn it*, as Judah did,

"THE SUCCESSFUL SON."

IV.

THE BLESSING OF ZEBULON; or, "THE SAILOR SON."

"Zebulon shall dwell at the haven of the sea: and he shall be for an haven of ships, and his border shall be unto Zidon."—GENESIS xlix. 13.

MANY people are what they are, not so much by anything which they themselves have done, as by the accidents or surroundings of their position. People who live among the mountains have a character of their own, as the Swiss and the Tyrolese, and the highlanders of the Scottish mountains in Europe, or the Green Mountain boys and the Rocky Mountain settlers in our own land. On the other hand, people who live on the seashore have their own separate and distinct character, as the fishermen of Nantucket, or the "Cape Cod folks," and the people from "down East," on the coast of Maine.

Now this son, Zebulon, who received his dying father's blessing, was one of these accidental characters. He was what he was, not because of anything which he himself had done, but he was simply and alone that which his surroundings made him. He took on the character of the country in which he lived, and was what he was, because his lot of land in Canaan was what it was.

You know that the lizard, called the chameleon, is remarkable for the fact that he takes on the color of the object on which he stands. If he is climbing up the trunk of a tree he will have a brown color. If he is nestling among the green leaves of the grass, he will appear green.

And some people in this world are very much like the chameleon. They reflect the objects which are around them.

This Zebulon was one of these accidental kind of people. He did not give character to the country in which he lived. His country imparted its character to him.

The territory which was assigned to the tribe, or clan, of Zebulon, extended on the northern part of Palestine, from the lake of Galilee to the Mediterranean Sea.

In this way the people of this tribe of Zebulon touched two kinds of life on the water: the inner boating life of the lake district of Galilee, and the outer or broader life of the Mediterranean Sea.

The hill country of the North was about them on every side, and the boundaries of the tribe extended to the inner waters of the lake, and to the outer waters of the ocean. I want to speak to you to-day about the blessing on

"THE SAILOR SON."

Sailors have a character of their own, and are what is called " cosmopolitan."

This is a big word, but it means a citizen of the whole world, one who is at home all over the world. A cosmopolitan is one who is at home in any part of the world. A provincial is one who is at home only in his own province or locality. City people are apt to be cosmopolitans; country people, on the other hand, are very apt to be provincial or narrow-minded.

The Jews were not fond of going about much. They liked to stay at home. The sea was always to them a terrible place. They did not like to travel over it. The 107th Psalm is filled with a terrified Jew's description of a storm at sea, and shows us the way in which the Jews regarded the ocean.

But the people of the tribe of Zebulon had to do with two kinds of water, the great ships on the ocean as well as the little boats on the Galilean lake, so that the children of Zebulon were acquainted with both the outer cosmopolitan world and the inner provincial world. The prophet Isaiah speaks in that beautiful lesson which is always read upon Christmas day of "the land of Zebulon by the way of the sea, beyond Jordan, in Galilee of the nations."

And thus it came to pass that the tribe of Zebulon had a country or provincial life, and it had a city or cosmopolitan life. It touched the lake country, and it touched the sea-coast country. And it was the character of its territory which gave character to the people who lived in it.

We learn three things from the blessing of Jacob upon Zebulon, the sailor or the cosmopolitan son.

I.

First.—We must remember that there are other people besides ourselves.

There is an old Russian proverb which says, "There are other people beyond the mountains." If you have ever lived in a place where there are mountains around you on every side, you will remember how these mountains seem to shut out the outside world, and seem to shut in the people who live in the valley all to themselves. Now it is a well-established fact, that people who never go away from home get into the way of becoming very narrow-minded. Not seeing other people they forget that there are other people and other ways of living, and judge everybody by their own standard of living. They forget that "there are other people beyond the mountains."

Artists, musicians, ministers, and newspaper men very frequently forget that there are other artists, musicians, ministers, and newspapers "beyond the mountains." They become like the inhabitants of the tribes of Israel which never touched either the waters of the inland lake, or the waters of the outer sea, as Zebulon did when he was "a haven for ships."

There was a French painter once who never went away from his own little town. He would not go to Paris to see the other painters' works, and did not care for any one's pictures but his own. One day he was lamenting to some friends who were in his study the great decline in the present world of painting.

"Zere air only zree great painters left in ze vorhld now," he said, with a sigh.

"Who are these?" asked his friend.

"*I am one*," said the village painter, placing

his hand upon his breast, " I have forgotten ze names of ze other two."

That painter had forgotten the first lesson of our subject to-day. He had forgotten that there are other people besides ourselves, other people who live beyond the mountains. When boys go away from their little primary schools to boarding-school or college, it seems very hard to them not to be treated in the same petted way in which they were treated at home. But we always find out our true position in life, not by thinking of what we are at home, but by finding out what we really are in the hands of our fellowmen. Many a little bantam rooster, crowing on his own hillock, has thought, when he never left his own barnyard, that he was the finest bird in all the world. But when he has mingled with the Shanghai lords of other barnyards, and has had a taste of the struggle of life, with torn comb and drooping feathers, he comes back to his own roost a humbler and a wiser fowl. We have learnt a great lesson in life, my dear children, when we have found out this Zebulon trait of character, this first lesson of our subject to-day, *that there are other people besides ourselves.*

II.

Secondly.—We are to remember that we are to carry blessings to others. It is a great sight to see the full-rigged ships with their square sails coming up the harbor to the dock, laden with every variety of cargo. Rice, fruits, East India goods, how many good things come to us over the sea from abroad. How many boys of the tribe of Zebulon must have watched to see the great galleys come over the blue Mediterranean Sea, and the little fishing-boats come lazily ashore across the lake of Galilee ! And how the caravans with camels and dromedaries must have gone through the country of Zebulon from the lake shore to the sea-side, carrying all sorts of commodities to the different towns and villages, which had been taken from the holds of the big ships and the little boats ! But the people of Zebulon, no doubt, sent back their own products in return for these goods received. And, my dear children, we must remember that we are not to receive cargoes of good things from others, and are then to go out to others, as ships go when they have nothing to carry, and take out simple ballast!

There is a great deal of this carrying of mere ballast to others who have brought rich and generous cargoes of good things to us. This world is fashioned on the principle of exchange. We give something in life, and we get something in return.

It will not do to be receiving continually good things from others, and then never to carry any blessing to them. If you go into a corn exchange or a broker's office, you will find that the principle of fair exchange is the great ruling principle of the business world.

"What will you give?" and
"What will you take?"

are the two first questions in the business man's catechism.

Now then, what are you giving to others in return for their blessings to you? The boys and girls of the tribe of Zebulon were very familiar with the things which came in trade from the ships across the sea. They were also very familiar with the things which went out in exchange trade. Children! What are you giving in exchange for the kindnesses you receive, as this sailor son, Zebulon, gave things as well as received them?

You say you are not yet of age; you cannot work or do a day's hard labor; you say you have to go to school and have no time left to do anything great for others! This is all true, but are you doing anything? You say what can we do?

Well! I will tell you.

You can love your parents and your brothers and sisters; you can be affectionate, kind, tender, and obedient. You can be willing to oblige; you can be ready to help those at home who have done so much for you. This is a good honest kind of exchange; such as the sailors of one country take out to the people of some other country.

All this you can give in exchange to your teachers and parents for all that they have done for you.

Dear children, do not make excuses all the time! Do not have reasons for not doing things when you are asked to do them at home. Some boys put logs, and stones, and stumps in the way whenever they are wanted to go on an errand. It is very often easier to do a thing oneself than to have to explain it over and over again to unwilling ears.

Remember the second lesson of this Zebulon sermon to-day.

Don't take ballast out in exchange for kindness received.

Remember that according to God's great law of exchange we are to carry blessings to others as well as have others bring their blessings to us!

III.

Thirdly, we must remember that other people can bring their blessings to us.

The older I grow the more deeply I feel that it is a great fault not to like people and to want to be with them.

Other people are necessary to us, and can bring us a blessing. Here was this tribe of Zebulon with its haven for ships. Other people came to Zebulon more than they did to the other tribes. They brought with them new ideas, and larger views of things, than they had in their own little tribe life.

There was a boy once at school named Carl, who quarrelled with all his companions, and made up his mind that he would cross off his list of friends every one he quarrelled with. At last, in the midst of the long winter term, he found out that he had quarrelled with them all, and that there was really not one left for him to play with.

At last one day the teacher found him looking through a knot-hole in the fence at the other boys playing ball in the play-ground.

"What are you doing, Carl?" asked his teacher.

"I am looking at the other boys play, sir," he replied.

"Why don't you play with them?" asked his teacher.

"Because I'm mad at them all, and vowed I wouldn't play with them!" said Carl.

"Well then," said his teacher, "why do you look at them play instead of playing by yourself."

Carl was silent a moment and then replied, "because I'm so awfully tired of myself."

We very soon get tired of ourselves in this world, my dear children, and it is a great help to us at times to feel that we can "play with" other people and can have them comfort us.

Do not despise other people; other people often bring great blessings to us, as they did to the tribe of Zebulon with his "haven for ships."

So you see Zebulon after all, with his "haven for ships," teaches us three lessons.

First.—There are other people besides ourselves.

Second.—We must carry blessings to other people.

Third.—Other people can carry their blessings to us.

Remember these lessons from the land of Zebulon.

Jesus said, "The field is the world—go ye therefore into all the world and preach the gospel to every creature."

When the apostles began to preach they began at Jerusalem, but their words went out into all the world, and have come down to us. Jesus did not come to save a province, he came to save the world.

To be large-minded and large-hearted, to avoid narrowness, bigotry, cant, and conceit, to remember others, to do for others, and not to be little, vain, or merely provincial in character, are some of the lessons we learn from the blessing on Zebulon,

"The Sailor Son."

V.

THE BLESSING OF ISSACHAR; or, "THE UNAMBITIOUS SON."

"Issachar is a strong ass couching down between two burdens: And he saw that rest was good, and the land that it was pleasant; and bowed his shoulder to bear, and became a servant unto tribute."—GENESIS xlix. 14.

THE dying Jacob did not mean to call his son a bad name when he said, "Issachar is a strong ass couching down between two burdens." The Jews never liked fast horses or fast ships. They were very much afraid of being run away with by horses and of being sunk by ships. So it came to pass that they used the ass instead of the horse, and did not venture upon the sea. In this way the ass came to be regarded as a great comfort and convenience.

They would load him up with packages in the panniers on his sides, and would then start him off on his journey. As the ass had no temptation to run away, he pleased the Jews, and came at last to stand for the idea of the family pack-horse. All the bundles—packages, travelling utensils, food, provender, bales of merchandise, satchels of clothing, furniture, women, children, and sick people—were put upon the shoulders of the ass.

The ass carried all the family loads. He was the pack-horse—the beast of burden for the family.

So then what Jacob meant by calling his son Issachar a strong ass was simply this:

He meant that Issachar would prove to be one of those persons who would go through life in a down-hearted, depressed, unambitious, poor-relation sort of way; that he would take what he could get, and would not expect great results; that he would labor and work and be the pack-horse of the family, and would be content with getting what he could out of the soil, and would leave the rest to others, and would give up all thought of making any better provision for himself.

And so these words of the dying Jacob came to be spoken, "He saw the land that it was good, and rest that it was pleasant, and bowed his shoulders to bear and became a servant unto tribute."

The lot given to the tribe of Issachar in the distribution of the land of Canaan extended from the river Jordan almost to the Mediterranean Sea. The lot of the tribe of Issachar was situated between the tribes of Zebulon and Manasseh, and consisted of a very rich and fertile soil.

The plain of Jezreel and the valley of Megiddo were found in the fruitful district of the tribe of Issachar. Agriculture, pasturage, and stock raising were the employment of the people of this tribe. It was a country which was very, very much like the fertile fields of Pennsylvania. Only the people of Issachar seemed to have no spirit. The judgment of Jacob upon the head of the tribe seems to have been realized in its later descendants. This down-heartedness and lack of spirit seems to have clung to them all their days.

They had no high ideals; they had no ambition; they were perfectly content with the ordinary life which they led among the sheep and the cattle. They did not care to rise. They saw the land that it was good, and rest that it was pleasant, and they bowed their shoulders to bear and became servants unto tribute.

We learn three lessons from the blessings of Jacob on this Issachar, "The unambitious son." If we want to get the most out of our nature we must remember,

I.

That there are times in life when we must lay our burdens down.

If you have ever seen a donkey with his two panniers, one on each side, you will understand how hard it must be for him to lie down and get any rest, or ease, or comfort with his burdens on his back.

THE UNAMBITIOUS SON. 73

A donkey can get no comfortable rest so long as his burdens are strapped upon his back.

And there are a great many people in this world who never take the burdens off their own shoulders. They lie down to sleep and rise up to their new duties with their burdens on. They never ease themselves of their little worries or frets, and never take their daily harness off.

You know how badly you feel when you have been sitting up all night with your clothes on, or when you have had a night's sleep on a lounge instead of going comfortably to bed for a good night's sleep. It is something like the feeling the cabman's horse had, when the cabman said that he never took him out of the shafts for fear he would fall down and never get into the shafts again.

"Issachar is a strong ass couching down between two burdens."

How many people there are, and how many children there are, who are all the time couching down between their burdens. They never lay down their loads; they never forget their cares. They go to bed with their worries and wake up with their worries, and have their petty little troubles tied about their necks all the time. There are housekeepers, and people who have plenty of statistics, and out-of-doors people who are always seen in the streets, and are always in a hurry, and walk very rapidly: and there are fretters and fumers, and whiners and whimperers, who are all the children of Issachar. They never take the panniers off their own bodies. They never lay their burdens down.

We ought never to refuse to carry our own burdens, my dear children, only we ought to take time to ease ourselves of our heavy loads, and unstrap the harness of our daily duties. Care is a divine blessing to us. God gives us cares, and if we ask him for strength whereby to carry them, he will give us his help so that our cares will seem light to us. But if we do not have real cares we generally have imaginary ones, and these are much harder to bear than the others. When God sends us troubles, he sends along with them grace whereby to bear them; when we give ourselves unnecessary troubles we have to bear them with our own strength alone.

The first lesson we learn from the blessing upon Issachar is this: that there are times in life when we must lay our burdens down.

If we want to get the most out of our nature we must remember,

II.

Secondly, that there are times in life, when we are tempted to think that what we have is good enough.

There are two kinds of ambition; one is good and the other is bad. There are two kinds of contentment, one is good and the other bad.

The bad ambition consists in being discontented with the lot in which God has placed us. The good ambition consists in being on the lookout for one's own improvement.

The good contentment consists in waiting patiently in the place in which it is evident that God has put us. The bad contentment consists in settling down to a lower position than that which we are capable of filling.

We must learn to be content with our lot; but we must also learn never to be content with our nature. We must learn, as the Catechism says, "to do our duty in that station of life to which it has pleased God to call us." But we must never rest content with our own weak nature: we must be trying every day to be better than we have been in the past.

But the whole trouble with Issachar was that, when he saw the fat, fair, and fertile valleys which were to be his share of Canaan, he said, "This will do—this is good enough." "He saw that rest was good and the land that it was pleasant, and he bowed his shoulder to bear and became a servant unto tribute."

THE UNAMBITIOUS SON. 77

Now, there are a great many people in the world who belong to the tribe of Issachar.

There are a great many boys and girls to-day who belong to the tribe of those who say, "This is good enough; this will do." There are a great many children to-day who have a lack of ambition, and do not try to get the best results out of their life and character. Their parents have done a great deal for them, and they think that they can go on and work on from the point where their parents have left off.

These are the boys and girls who are content to be second-best at school; who do not desire to "go up higher," but who think things are good enough as they are.

"Where do you stand in your class, Bobby?" asked a gentleman once of a little boy.

"Next to head," replied Bobby.

"Why, that is very good," answered the gentleman; "I am glad to see you are so high up."

Afterwards this gentleman found out that

there were three boys in this class, and that while Bobby was next to head, at the same time he was next to tail. But that contented Bobby, because he belonged to the tribe of Issachar. He was one of the boys who said that what he had was good enough.

I was reading the other day General Grant's history of his own life. It is a wonderful book, and describes the great events of his life in a quiet, unpretending way, as if there was nothing very remarkable about them.

But the wonderful thing about Grant's life was this, that at the age of forty, when he was a tanner at Galena, and enlisted for the war, he resolved to *make himself over* on the *pattern of a better man* than he had been before. His life shows us the weak points in his early career, and it was because he recognized these weak spots in his early life that he knew just how to make himself strong in the places in which he had formerly been weak.

Now one of his early weak points was this very point of our subject. You would not

THE UNAMBITIOUS SON. 79

believe it, but he shows clearly himself that when he was a boy he belonged to this very tribe of Issachar. He was one of those who said, "This will do—this is good enough."

When he was a cadet at West Point, he says, he was always some distance from the top of the class, and some distance from the tail.

But after a while he graduated out of the tribe of the children of Issachar, and was never content until he had gained the most out of every duty which was laid upon him, and out of every position in which he was placed.

Remember, then, my dear children, this second lesson of our subject to-day. If we want to get the most out of our nature we must remember that there are times in life when we are tempted to think that what we have is good enough.

If we want to get the most out of our nature we must remember,

III.

Thirdly, that we can never be helpers to others while we are slaves to ourselves.

Think of the difference between being a slave to others and of being free to do our own will.

In Mrs. Stowe's wonderful book, "Uncle Tom's cabin," there is the story of a slave mother, Eliza—flying away, across the Ohio river, filled with blocks of ice, in winter time, to try and get up to Canada, where she could be free and be a true mother to her children.

It is a very thrilling story; the officers are after her and the bloodhounds are after her, but she hurries on to get the river between her and her pursuers, so that she may fly away to a country where she can be the real mother to her children, simply because then she will not be a slave herself.

And, my dear children, if we make slaves of ourselves to our own cares and worries and low views of things, we can never be helpers to others.

Because Issachar had no ambition to be better than his brethren he became poorer and worse off than they. They made a packhorse of him, and put their bundles on him, and in this way "he bowed his shoulders to bear and became a servant unto tribute."

Issachar was the "poor relation" of the twelve sons of Jacob.

He was not bad like Simeon and Levi; he was not prosperous like Judah; he was not good like Joseph.

He simply "didn't get on." He was what is called "a ne'er do well."

Now, the trouble with this kind of people is not that they are poor and down-hearted. The trouble with them is that they keep forever talking about their misery.

They settle down at last like Issachar of old and keep the burdens strapped on them all the time, and succumb to their surroundings—instead of rising above their surroundings.

My dear children, life is a great struggle and is filled with hard problems. After you have grown a little older, you will surely find this lesson out.

Therefore let us try to make the best out of life and its surroundings, and not the worst; and let us avoid the mistake of Issachar, Jacob's down-hearted, depressed, unambitious son.

These then are the lessons which we learn from the blessing of Issachar:

If we want to get the most out of our nature we must remember,

1st. That there are times in life when we must lay our burdens down.

2d. That there are times in life when we are tempted to think that what we have is good enough.

3d. That we can never be helpers to others while we are slaves to our own selves.

I do not think this was much of a blessing —this blessing upon Issachar. But the trouble was not with Jacob who gave the blessing; the trouble was with Issachar; *there wasn't anything to bless in him.*

The whole trouble was with this lucky-go-easy, unambitious son.

My dear children, let us all move our tents outside the boundaries of the tribe of Issachar, so that we may never deserve the judgment which was pronounced upon Issachar,

"THE UNAMBITIOUS SON."

VI.

THE BLESSING ON DAN, "THE DECEITFUL SON."

"Dan shall be a serpent by the way, an adder in the path, that biteth the horse-heels, so that his rider falleth backward. I have waited for thy salvation, O Lord."—GENESIS xlix. 17, 18.

THERE is an old Turkish proverb which says, "Trust not the whiteness of his turban; he bought the soap on credit."

This means that even the Turk's clean turban is clean through deceit; the very soap which was bought to wash it clean was not paid for.

Deceit is a terrible stain to get into one's blood. It seems at times as if there was no such thing as ever getting it out of the nature when it once gets in. It takes a very firm grip, and holds on from generation to generation.

Here in this family of Jacob's it took three or four generations to get the stain of deceit out of the blood.

First of all, Jacob's mother, Rebecca, deceived Isaac, her husband, and secured the first born's blessing for Jacob, when it belonged to his brother Esau.

Then Jacob deceived his father, and his Uncle Laban, and his brother Esau, and after him his son Dan became known for his mean, and tricky, and deceitful ways.

And so it came to pass that the act of deceitfulness on the part of Jacob's mother, Rebecca, worked its way out into his life and character, and through him into the character of this tribe of Dan,—which tribe was always known for its habits of deceit, its great man, Samson, being the most mischievous, and tricky, and deceitful of all its children.

I was reading in the paper, the other day, a story about a little newsboy, who, to sell his paper, told a lie. The matter came up in Sunday-school. "Would you tell a lie for three cents?" asked the teacher of one of the boys.

"No, ma'am!" answered Dick very decidedly. "For a dollar?"—"No, ma'am!"—"For a thousand dollars?" Dick was staggered. A thousand dollars looked big. It would buy lots of things. While he was thinking another boy behind him roared out, "No, ma'am!"—"Why not?" asked the teacher. "Because," said the boy, "when the thousand dollars is all gone, and all the things they have got with them are gone too, the lie is there all the same." That boy had got hold of the truth which the character of Dan teaches us. *Deceit sticks.* Now, this tribe of Dan, whose blessing or judgment, we have for our thoughts to-day, was the little State, the Rhode Island of the united Kingdom of Israel.

It was a little tribe, with a very limited territory, and was situated to the north of the Sea of Galilee, right under the shadow of the snowy sides of Mount Hermon. The tribe of Dan was one which quarrelled a great deal, and which very soon in its history fell into idolatry. Samson, the strong man of the Old Testament, belonged to this tribe;

but it did not have many great men, or achieve any distinction in the history of the Kingdom.

It is the only tribe whose name is omitted from the list of those which are sealed in the book of the Revelation of St. John with the twelve thousand elect ones.

"Of the tribe of Reuben *was* sealed twelve thousand. Of the tribe of Judah *was* sealed twelve thousand." And all the other tribes are named in this catalogue as having twelve thousand souls saved in Heaven. But Dan is never mentioned. The tribe of Dan is omitted altogether; there were none sealed from this tribe at all. This is a very striking thought of the evil of deceit.

Our subject to-day is the warning from "The deceitful son." What do we learn from Dan?

I.

First of all we learn that deceit is a remnant of the beast nature within us.

When the immortal Sidney was told that

he might save his life by telling a falsehood and denying his hand-writing, he answered, "When God hath brought me into a dilemma, in which I must assert a lie, or lose my life, he gives me a clear indication of my duty; which is to prefer death to falsehood."

But no animal would prefer death to deceit, unless it be a highly educated dog.

Beasts have an instinct within them to save themselves at all hazards, and deceive on purpose to save themselves.

A cat deceives by her stealthy tread; a bird deceives — like the curlew and the marsh-bird when they want to save their nests. A hedgehog will fall over and make believe that he is dead on purpose to deceive a passer-by, and a "possum up the gum-tree" will hang by the hour as if he were dead. To "play possum" has come, with the colored people of the South, to mean to deceive. "Don't trust him, massah," a slave boy would call out to his master, "don't trust him. He's only playing possum."

If any of you children have ever read that

very interesting and amusing book, "Uncle Remus," you will remember how Uncle Remus used to tell the little children about "Brer Rabbit," and "Brer Fox," and "Brer Bear," and "Sis Cow." "Brer Rabbit" was always the one who deceived the other animals, and got them into all sorts of scrapes with the "Tar Baby," and all the other pranks.

The colored people in the old slave days which are described in "Uncle Remus," always thought of "Brer Rabbit," with his long ears and funny looking face as the embodiment of all that was tricky and mischievous. The Rabbit was the Dan of all the animal tribes. He deceived the other animals, so that they were always made sport of by the rabbit.

Deceit is right enough when we find it among animals, for it is one of their natural weapons of defence; but whenever it crops out in our nature, we ought to rise up and put it down, and stamp on it, as we would upon a snake in the grass or fire among shavings. Deceit is a remnant of the old serpent nature, the snake within us, and we ought to crush it out whenever it appears within us, or it will grow until it becomes to us a dreadful curse.

II.

Secondly. — We learn from the blessing upon Dan that deceitfulness is the trade-mark of the old serpent.

When we say the old serpent, we mean Satan, the father of lies. Jesus said of the devil, " when he speaketh a lie he speaketh of his own, for he is a liar and the father of lies."

Perjury and deceitfulness are the signs of a rotten character. I was reading the other day about a certain Ludovicus, who was king of Burgundy. He was taken prisoner, but was given his liberty upon promising not to make war again. Upon receiving his freedom, he raised a stronger army than before. He was again overcome, and lost all. His eyes were plucked out, and these words were branded upon his forehead: "This man was saved by clemency, and lost by perjury." His perjury was the trade-mark of his character, and lost him his life.

Honesty on the other hand is the trademark of all God's children, and always brings its own reward with it.

In the days of the late rebellion there was a young volunteer who was expecting daily to be ordered to the seat of war. One day his mother gave him an unpaid bill with money, and asked him to pay it. When he returned home that night she said, " Did you pay the bill?"—"Yes," he answered. In a few days the bill was sent in a second time. "I thought," said she to her son, " that you paid this."—"I really don't remember, mother; you know I've had so many things on my mind."—"But you said you did."—"Well," he answered, "if I said I did, I did." He went away, and the mother took the bill herself to the store. The young man had been known in town all his life, and what opinion was held of him this will show.

"I am quite sure," she said, "that my son paid this some days ago; he has been very busy since, and has quite forgotten about it; but he told me that day he had, and says if he said then that he had, he is quite sure that he did."—"Well," said the man, "I forgot about it; but if he ever said he did, he did."

This trade-mark of honesty or deceit is found in us all. Like the trade-mark of Sheffield steel, or Gorham metal, or the mark of "Tiffany's" silver, or the water-mark in the paper of "Crane's" and "Weston's" celebrated Dalton paper mills, the trade-mark of honesty or deceit is stamped upon our character and our faces, and marks us as the children of God or of the Devil.

III.

Thirdly.—Deceitfulness brings a curse to the person who uses it.

It is said, you know, that curses are like chickens, they come home to roost. If you have ever watched a lot of chickens coming back to the hen-house at night, you will remember how slowly, but how surely, they find their way back.

Now they stop a moment to scratch and pick up bits of food, and then they cluck and crow and chirrup to one another, but sooner or later they always get back to the hen-house before the sun goes down.

Sometimes our Dan-like habits of deceit bring the evil returns in a very short space of time.

Some years ago a young aspirant for office in Iowa drove up to a hotel, alighted and engaged a room. He desired his trunk taken to his room; and, seeing a man passing whom he supposed to be the porter, he imperiously ordered him to take it up. The porter charged him twenty-five cents, which he paid with a marked quarter, worth only twenty cents. He then said, "You know Gov. Grimes?"—"O yes, sir!"—"Well, take my card to him, and tell him I wish an interview at his earliest convenience."—"I am Gov. Grimes, at your service, sir."—"You—I—

that is, my dear sir, I beg—a—a thousand pardons!"—" None needed at all, sir," replied Gov. Grimes. "I was rather favorably impressed with your letter, and had thought you well suited for the office specified; but, sir, any man who would swindle a working man out of a paltry five cents would defraud the public treasury, had he an opportunity. Good evening, sir!"

The older I grow, my dear children, the more truly I feel that it is always better, wiser, and happier for us to be honest and straight-forward in everything we do, than to be tricky, underhanded, and deceitful. There is always a reward about honesty; there is always a curse about deceit. We always get punished when we try to deceive.

No words are truer than those of the poet Scott, in his poem of "Marmion,"—

"O what a tangled web we weave,
When first we practice to deceive."

Deceit is the trade-mark of Satan, and all Satan's tools are two-edged: they hurt the person who uses them as well as the person against whom they are used.

A young man went one evening to consult his minister respecting the situation which he filled in a large drapery establishment. His master required him to tell falsehoods about the goods, and to cheat the customers whenever he could do so; and his conscience told him that this was wrong. His minister advised him to refuse to act thus dishonestly. "I shall lose my place," said the young man. —"Then lose your place; don't hesitate a moment."—"I engaged for a year, and my year is not out."—"No matter; you are ready to fulfil your engagement. Did you engage to deceive, to cheat, and lie?"—"O no, not at all."—"Then certainly you need have no hesitation through fear of forfeiting your place. If he sends you away because you will not do such things for him, you will know him to be a bad man, from whom you may be glad to be separated."—"I have no place to go to, and he knows it."—"I would go anywhere, do anything, dig potatoes, black boots, sweep the streets for a living, sooner than yield to such temptations."—"I don't think I can stay there; but I don't know what to do or where to look."—"Look to God first, and trust in Him. Do you think He will let you suffer, because out of regard to His commandments, you have lost your place? Never. Such is not His way. Ask Him to guide you." The young man acted upon the advice given. He was dismissed from his situation, but he found another, where he established a character for integrity and promptness, and entered afterward into business for himself. He prospered, and is now a man of extensive property and high respectability.

Depend upon it, my dear children, there is more power in the blessing of honesty than there is in the curse of deceit.

IV.

Fourthly.—Deceitfulness never brings us God's way of peace.

When we are tempted to lie and deceive,

and play the part of the serpent in the path, it is because we think we can gain some advantage for ourselves, or can get ourselves out of some trouble. But we can never get good results by using bad means. We can never get straight ends by using crooked means. "That which is crooked cannot be made straight."

There was a boy once who made up his mind that every time he did an unfair or dishonest act, or told a lie, he would drive a nail into a post by the barn.

At the end of six months' time he found that one-third of the post was covered with nails.

"Now Tom," said his father, "every time you win a victory over your temptation *draw out a nail* with the claw end of the hammer."

So Tom went to work with the nail extractor. In six months' time he called his father to look at the post. "See, father," said Tom, "I've got all the nails out at last."

"Yes," replied his father, "you've got the nails all out, but the scars remain, you see."

The post was black with holes where the nails had been.

And so it is with us, my dear children, every time we repent of our sins, we draw the sin out, like the nail out of the post—but *the scars of the holes remain.*

But God's way of peace is not to let us have any scars at all. And this is much better than our way of deceiving and then repenting of our deceit.

If you get into scrapes, dear children, do not lie to get out of them. Walk out of them in an honest way. Don't be like the serpent in the path, which biteth the horse-heels so that the rider falls backward.

These then are the lessons which we learn from Jacob's blessing upon Dan.

1st. Deceit is a remnant of the beast nature within us.

2d. Deceit is the trade-mark of the devil.

3d. Deceit brings a curse to the person who uses it.

4th. Deceit never brings us God's way of peace.

Poor Dan, his was a worm-eaten, rotten character. He was a deceitful, dishonest son.

If you have ever seen an old ship-wrecked hulk on the sea-shore, you will remember how the timbers and joists were worm-eaten, until they looked as soft as a sponge; you could knock them into a hundred bits with the stick in your hand.

Well! in the same way a rotten and deceitful nature never can be trusted! A worm-eaten timber is the very image of a worm-eaten character.

What a description is this text of ours of a deceitful nature:

"Dan shall be a serpent in the way; an adder in the path, that biteth the horse-heels, so that the rider falleth backward."

And I suppose it was because Jacob had learned that it was better to do right and leave the results in God's hands, than it was to be crafty, and tricky, and deceitful, that he added these final words,—

"I have waited (or I have learned to wait) for *thy* salvation, O Lord."

VII.

THE BLESSING OF GAD, or, "THE PERSEVERING SON."

"Gad, a troop shall overcome him: but he shall overcome at the last."—GENESIS xlix. 19.

IT is a great art to know how to work one's way through a crowd. We get jostled back and forth as we try to work our way to the heart of the crowd, and at times it seems as if we should surely perish in the surging, crowding mass of our fellow-men.

I was riding some time ago in the cars with an ex-Governor of Massachusetts, and we fell into a talk about the best way of working oneself out to the front in a great concourse of men.

My friend the Governor said, "the secret of it all is not to be in a hurry. One must not crowd or push or be in a hurry. One must wait until there comes an opening, and then quietly sidle into the opening; wait there a moment, then slip a step forward, wait again, and in this way quietly work forward to the front.

As my friend the Governor had been a very successful man in politics, I thought his advice was very good, and ever since that day I have known just how to work my way through what seemed at first sight to be an impenetrable crowd of men.

Now this description of how to work one's way through a crowd is the exact description of this persevering son Gad, whose blessing we are to consider to-day. His father's words were, "Gad, a troop shall overcome him—*but he shall overcome at the last.*"

This tribe of Gad was situated on the other side of the river Jordan, and was what was called one of the "trans-Jordanic tribes."

The tribes of Dan — Manasseh — Reuben, and Gad were the tribes which were situated on the eastern side of the River Jordan. Somehow or other the other tribes looked down on them, because they were situated on the other side of the river—just as in London people think to-day that the Surrey side of the river Thames is not as respectable as the other side. Somehow or other, these "trans-Jordanic tribes" were looked down upon by the other tribes as if they were not as respectable as those who lived on the western side of the river. Well! This tribe of Gad was the easternmost of all the tribes. In its territory were found Ramoth Gilead, Jabesh Gilead, the brook Jabbok where Jacob crossed to meet his brother Esau—and that historic place called Peniel, where he wrestled with the angel until the break of day. To the east of this tribe of Gad were the wild aborigines of the country, called the Zuzims and Zam-zummims.

These wild Tartar-like tribes were continually making attacks upon the newly settled tribes of Israel.

The tribe of Gad fared badly in all their border warfare. It became like that part of Scotland over which the Highlanders and the

Lowlanders were continually fighting. It was like Belgium, the battle field of Europe, in the days of the Emperor Charles the Fifth and of the first Napoleon.

These Zuzims, or Zam-zummims would come down in a troop upon them and drive them across the river Jordan. But the people of this tribe of Gad were very persevering in character. They would never give up the fight, and though at the first they were driven off, at the last they prevailed and drove the intruders out of their territory. And in this way it happened that the far-off prophecy of old Jacob was fulfilled. "Gad, a troop shall overcome him: but he shall overcome at the last."

We are to consider to-day the blessing which comes upon the persevering son. And by the persevering son we mean that son who knows how to work his way through a crowd to the front; the son who is not overcome by a multitude, but who, though a troop may overcome him, overcomes all at last.

It is very surprising to see what perseverance will do in conquering one's own faint-heartedness and in overcoming a troop of difficulties at the last.

I was reading the other day one of Percy's stories about the perseverance of a Saracen princess, and how she was rewarded at the last.

The story was as follows: Gilbert Becket, who was afterwards a flourishing citizen, was in his youth a soldier in the crusades, and being taken prisoner became a slave to a Saracen prince. He obtained the confidence of his master, and was loved by the prince's daughter.

After some time he effected his escape; but the lady with her loving heart followed him. She knew but two words of the English language, "London" and "Gilbert," and by repeating the first she obtained a passage on a vessel, arrived in England, and found her way to the metropolis. She then took to the other word, and went from street to street pronouncing the word, "Gilbert," Gilbert," wherever she went. A crowd collected about her asking a thousand questions, and to all she had but one answer, "Gilbert," "Gilbert!" At last her determination to go through every street brought her to that one in which he who had won her heart in slavery was living in a prosperous condition. The crowd attracted the family to the window; his servant recognized her, and Gilbert Becket at last wedded his far come princess, with her solitary fond word.

"Gad, a troop shall overcome him: but he shall overcome at the last."

What do we learn from the blessing on the persevering son?

I.

First of all we learn that perseverance is developed by the exercise of a strong will.

There is a process at the photographer's office which is called developing the negative. The plate, or negative as it is called, when the picture is taken, is brought out into the open sunlight under a glass, and in this way the power of the sun's rays brings out, or develops, the details of the picture.

And, my dear children, perseverance is like a photographer's negative. It does not come to a picture at once; it has to be developed and brought out by the power of one's own will. A strong will develops the power of perseverance as the sunlight develops the photograph. The most of us are not persevering by nature; if we have perseverance at all, it generally comes as it came to Gad, by experience. "A troop shall overcome him: but he shall overcome at the last."

When Doctor Carey, the celebrated missionary, was a boy, he tried one day to climb a tree; but his foot slipped and he fell to the ground, breaking his leg by the fall. This accident confined him to his bed many weeks, and caused him much suffering. But when his broken limb was healed, the first thing he did was to go and climb that same tree again, until he got to the top.

Perseverance always wins in the race of

life. Not to give up easily: not to grow discouraged and abandon one's work: not to turn aside from a central purpose in life, for the sake of some passing whim, will surely give us the victory.

Among the different games and races at Athens, there was one in which every contestant carried a burning torch in his hand. The runner who arrived at the end without having his torch extinguished obtained the prize.

If we light the torch of perseverance and keep it at the head of the race of life, we shall be pretty sure to win.

"Hard pounding! Hard pounding, gentlemen," said the Duke of Wellington, at the battle of Waterloo, "but we will see who can pound the longest."

And the side which pounded the longest was the side which won.

As I write this sermon, I look up from my desk at a picture of the last charge of Napoleon's Guard at Waterloo, which hangs before me. They did their best, and tried their hardest to win the day, but the hard pounding of the other side was too much for the broken French Guard. The battle of Waterloo was won to the English not by brilliant generalship, but simply by long and persevering pounding.

II.

Secondly.—Perseverance is the sign of a reserve of nature.

A reserve of any kind is a great thing to have. A reserve in bank is a great thing to fall back upon. A reserve stock of strength in life, a reserve supply in an army, are all very serviceable in the matter of helping us to win the victory.

I remember a young minister who, when he left the Divinity School, and was ordained, wrote a wonderful sermon filled with power and wisdom. But when he came to write his second sermon he found that he had said all he had to say in his first sermon. He could think of nothing more to say. He walked up and down his room, troubled with the alternative of saying nothing that was true, or saying nothing that was new. He had either to write poor stuff, or repeat what he had already said. At last he went to see his old minister and preceptor, to talk this matter out with him.

"I can't tell what's the matter," said the young minister. "Both John, my companion, and I can't write a second sermon without saying over again what we have already said in our first sermon. What is the matter with us?"

"Matter with you?" replied the old minister. "Matter with you—why there's only one thing the matter with you. You and John are both bright boys, but the trouble is *you have both got all your goods in your shop window.*"

What this old minister meant was that there was no reserve of strength to these young men. All their capital was in their first sermon. A store, you know, which has all its goods in a show-case or in a show-window, and has empty shelves inside, has not got much capital with which to carry on the business.

But perseverance in fitting up the unseen shelves inside with goods, will give a storekeeper great strength when his shop window is exhausted.

A good reserve on hand will help a bank to fight its way through a business panic. And a good reserve of strength of character will help us in the day of trial and temptation, and nothing shows that we have a reserve of nature so surely as this Gad-like quality of hanging on through thick and thin, and never giving up at all; this all-conquering faculty of perseverance.

When the late Lord Beaconsfield first entered the English House of Commons, he was such a fantastically dressed looking fop, and was beside this the son of a Jew, that the entire house laughed at him when he sat down, after making his opening speech.

As he took his seat amidst the jeers and derision of the house, he rose again upon his feet and exclaimed, as he lifted up his right hand to the roof, "You laugh at me now, I know, but the time will come when you will be glad to hear me."

When he was a boy, he said, when asked what he meant to be in life, "I want to be the prime minister of England, and the prime minister I shall become."

"Gad, a troop shall overcome him: but he shall overcome at the last."

III.

Thirdly, Perseverance is the sign of concentrativeness of purpose.

Concentrativeness is a big word of five syllables, but it is an easy word to spell, and all words which are easy to spell are easy to understand. To concentrate, is to bring many opposite things together, so as to give force to the whole. Concentrativeness is the act of bringing many things together, so as to get a strong result from their combined action.

Here is a story which explains what I mean by concentrativeness:

A little boy was once watching a large building, as the workmen from day to day carried up bricks and mortar.

"My son," said his father, "you seem very much interested in the bricklayers. Do you think of learning the trade?"

"No," he replied. "I was thinking what a little thing a brick is, and what great houses are built by laying one brick on another."

"Well, my boy," answered his father, "so it is in all the great works of life. The bricks which make up a great building like this are not dumped on by cart-loads. They are placed on very carefully, brick by brick. And the duties and habits which go to make up a successful life are laid one by one upon a human character."

Now, perseverance is the sign that we are concentrating our powers upon a definite piece of work before us, so as to succeed in that which we have undertaken.

You all know what a great and good man John Wesley, the founder of Methodism, was.

One day John Wesley's father said to his wife, while patiently teaching her boy one of his school lessons, "Why do you take so much time with that stupid boy?"

"Because," replied the mother, "nineteen times won't do. If I tell him but nineteen times, all my labor is lost; but the twentieth time secures the object."

It was the power of that mother in concentrating her energies upon John Wesley which made him the man he afterwards became.

John Wesley's mother centered all her powers upon her boy to make a man of him, and the result of all her energies was "John Wesley."

Now, my dear children, remember these three lessons about Gad, the son who knew how to push his way to the front; the son who knew how to drive back his enemies, even though at the first he himself had been driven back.

I. Perseverance is developed by the exercise of a strong will.

II. Perseverance is the sign of a reserve of nature.

III. Perseverance is the sign of concentrativeness of purpose.

At a certain battle, an officer who had been doing good service came up to General Sir Charles Napier, and said, "Sir Charles, we have taken a standard." The general looked at him, but made no reply, and turning round, began to speak to some one else, upon which the officer repeated, "Sir Charles, we have taken a standard." The general turned sharp round upon him and said, "Then take another."

So I say to you to-day, if you have gained one victory by perseverance, then go and gain another, and in saying this end my sermon about

"GAD, THE PERSEVERING SON."

VIII.

THE BLESSING OF ASHER, or THE "SELF-INDULGENT SON."

"Out of Asher his bread shall be fat, and he shall yield royal dainties."—GENESIS xlix. 20.

NEAR old St. Paul's church on Third Street in Philadelphia, there used to be a restaurant, in front of which fat green turtles were deposited upon their backs.

I can remember as a little boy, when going to Sunday-school, how we used to stop and look at those green turtles squirming their feet, and rolling their heads, and trying in every way to get on their feet again.

But as the superintendent of the school was strict, and as the boys who were late had to go up and turn over a big card with the words on it, "I am late,"—we never used to get a long enough look at those green turtles—predestined to be made into turtle soup.

There were good, bad and indifferent boys who used to go to that old Sunday-school. Bishop Odenheimer and Edwin Forest, Henry George, the political economist, and Owen Faucett, the actor, George C. Thomas, and many others used to attend that famous school, and stand up before the superintendent and recite texts and verses, and sing with Mr. Farr who used to play on the melodeon.

But about these turtles, as I was saying, there they used to lie on the flat of their backs, the very picture of fat, easy-going, luxurious creatures. There was a shoe store, and a gun store, and a cake store, where they had cinnamon buns for a cent a piece, and there was this green turtle place, all on Third Street. Well! I have never thought of those fat, unctuous looking turtles from that day to this, but, somehow, when I came to write this sermon about Asher, the luxurious self-indulgent son, in some strange way, my mind went back again over all those years to the green turtles which used to tempt us to wait at the corner of Third and Walnut Streets. The words, "Out of Asher his bread shall be fat, and he shall yield royal dainties," have a very luxurious sound. They seem to tell us of what is called good living, of state dinners, and of delights of the table.

I confess it sounds to me as if it had to do in some way with the sin of gluttony; and one of the first things I ever remember in my life connected with the thought of self-indulgence and gluttony was the sight of those green turtles on their backs, at Third and Walnut Streets, when I was a little boy, hurrying along so that I might not have to turn over that dreadful card,

"I am late,"

in the presence of the superintendent at old St. Paul's Sunday-school.

Now self-indulgence, luxury, gluttony; and caring only for what are called the good things of life, are habits which will surely coil the devil's chain about us, and make us his captives. And I suppose in this way these green turtles came to my mind to stand for the sin of gluttony. There is nothing wrong or sinful in green turtles themselves or about having them for turtle-soup.

It is only when we make eating and drinking the chief end of life, and spend all our time in thinking about the delights and pleasures of good living and eating, that green turtles come to be associated with the thought of gluttons and the sins of gluttony.

Some years ago when I was in Paris I went to see a set of pictures called the Seven Castles of the Devil. They represented what are called the seven deadly sins. The seven deadly sins are:

I. Pride.
II. Covetousness.
III. Lust.
IV. Anger.
V. Gluttony.
VI. Envy.
VII. Sloth.

I shall never forget the picture of gluttony.

Bottles of wine, cakes, pies, glaces, jellies, meats, fruit, vegetables, birds, fish, and all sorts of things to be eaten were all crowding their way around the castle where the glutton was imprisoned, and were determined to conquer the castle and kill the glutton within, by making him eat too much.

Now to be a glutton is nothing less than to be a human pig. The one end and aim of a pig is to eat and fill himself with food and then go and lie down and sleep it off. A pig doesn't care for anything but the swill trough and the mud. A pig never thinks about the blue sky or the green grass or any of the beauties of nature. All a pig ever thinks of is to get back to his swill-trough once more.

And there are a great many people in the world, my dear children, who act as if they did not care for very much more besides the delights of the dinner-table. When we see children at parties stuffing themselves at the table, and then hiding away nuts and cakes and sugar-plums in their pockets, and when we see grown up people, who ought to set children a better example, doing the same thing around a party table, it makes us feel that the sin of gluttony or self-indulgence is a sin which links those who indulge in it to those uninteresting animals who grunt, and live in what is called a sty.

I want to-day, my dear children, to warn you against the evil habit of self-indulgence. If we get into the way of always looking out for "royal dainties," and for "fat" places, like this luxurious son Asher, we will become spoiled and selfish and pampered, and wayward men and women. Spoiled children are dreadful to have about the house; and self-indulgent Asher-like children, who are always on the look-out for having the best of everything and taking care of No. 1 at all times and in all places, are a nuisance.

So then, let us come back to Asher, the self-indulgent and luxurious son, and let us find out what lessons we can learn from him.

If we would avoid the evil habit of self-indulgence we must remember these three things:

I.

First, we must try to put something into life, and not merely try to get something out of life. This tribe of Asher was situated near the Mediterranean Sea, afar up to the North. Mt. Lebanon and Mt. Hermon stood guard at the North, and Mt. Carmel was at the South, looking out over the Mediterranean Sea. It was all right in these people of the tribe of Asher to raise fat crops and luxurious vines. All these things are well enough in their place. It is only when we make them the chief end and aim of life, and live entirely for them, that we run the risk of developing within us the evil habit of self-indulgence.

David Garrick, the celebrated actor, once showed his friend, Dr. Johnson, his fine house, gardens, statues, and pictures at Hampton Court.

As the Doctor was about to leave, he shook his friend's hand, and said, "Ah! David, David, these are the things which make a death-bed terrible."

My dear children, we cannot get out of life the happiness we want unless first of all we put some happiness into the life of others. If we go about continually thinking how we can make our friends and our position and our duties in life serve us and yield us "royal dainties," we will lay up for ourselves a miserable old age in the midst of our luxurious self-indulgence.

Depend upon it, my dear children, we will get out of life the full crop of that which we put into life. That which we sow we shall surely reap. If you have a garden and sow flower seeds, and corn and vegetables and potatoes, you will reap the fruit of these in the Fall time. But if you plant flat-irons or iron nails, nothing will ever come up out of them, simply because there is nothing to come; they have got no hidden life in them.

And in the same way, my dear children, if we put good seed into life, if we plant good habits and sound principles in our nature, we will reap a rich harvest in the growth of our character in after days. But if we are only like Asher, continually on the look-out for fat things and royal dainties, and make the idea of the green turtles, the ruling idea of our life, we will be forever caught in the chain of luxury and self-indulgence.

If we would avoid the habit of self-indulgence, we must remember

II.

Secondly.—That we must keep our bodies under, so as not to become the slaves of greed.

A curb-bit is a great thing to have upon a restive, ungovernable horse. It holds him down and stops his waywardness as nothing else can do. And a curb-bit on our passions and evil habits is a great help to us in the way of teaching us how to submit to the will of our better nature.

St. Paul says in one place, "Walk in the Spirit and ye shall not fulfil the lusts of the flesh." He means by this, that if we do not walk in the way of temptation we shall not feel the power of temptation. If we keep under our feet the thoughts and appearances of evil, we will not be subject to their power. And in another place he says, "I keep under my body, and bring it into subjection, lest that by any means when I had preached to others I myself should be a castaway."

This is a great principle for us all in life to learn. It means that St. Paul had learned how to use the curb-bit on his passions, and so he rode his own horse, instead of having his horse run away with him.

As I sit at my desk, up here among the Berkshire Hills, I often look out on the road to Dalton, with the blue hills covered with snow around it. Along this road go droves of cattle, sheep and pigs to be killed.

The poor things mostly go along the road in droves very quietly. But every now and then a cross bull appears who is led by a rope which is tied to a brass ring in his nose, or a fierce pig, who looks ugly and keeps his ears up, is led by a rope around his hind leg. Sometimes these animals perform a dance in the road, and go round and round the man in the centre, like the spokes of a wheel around the hub. But the man with the cord tied to the bull's nose and the pig's hind leg generally gets the better of the animals, and after a little while they go on again, very quietly.

And I have often thought, my dear children, how like this man with the rope, we have to tie up in this same way certain fierce passions and habits within us. If we can get the ring through the nose of anger, or can get a rope around the leg of our self-indulgence, and can give these bad habits a pull when they begin to carry on and give us trouble, what a great thing it is for our soul's growth.

If our bad habits get the upper hand and run away with us, we fall: but if we can keep them under, then we shall be able to win in the great fight of life, and we shall be made conquerors by the grace which God has given us, whereby to resist temptation.

III.

Thirdly.—We must remember that self-indulgence creeps upon us unconsciously, and must be fought to the bitter end. When we come to think about it we shall find that all the seven deadly sins are contained within this sin of self-indulgence. All the seven castles of the devil are after all enclosed within this one.

Self-indulgence makes us

    1st. Proud.   2d. Covetous.
    3d. Lustful.   4th. Angry.
    5th. Envious. 6th. Slothful.

Indeed it seems as if this Asher-like desire for bread that "shall be fat," and for "royal dainties," this determination always to be on the lookout for one's own little pet self, were the mother of all the remaining bad habits within us. We are selfish, very often, before we know it. It is natural for us to want to be self-indulgent, but if we do not fight against this evil habit it will ruin our nature and make us to be despised of our fellow-men. I have sometimes watched the lobsters on the rocks at the seashore, and they have taught me a lesson. When they have been left high and dry among the rocks they have not sense and energy enough to work their way back to the sea, but wait on the rocks for the sea to come to them. If the sea does not come, they remain on the rocks and are caught, or die where they are, while all the time only the slightest exertion on their part would enable them to reach the tumbling waves below. And unless we arouse ourselves and fight to the bitter end this lazy self-indulgence which comes creeping over us, we will be made captive by those fat things and royal dainties which captured the glutton in the castle of self-indulgence in the painting I spoke about, in the series of pictures of the Seven Castles of the Devil.

These are the three lessons then which we learn from Asher, the self-indulgent son.

1. We must try to put something into life, and not merely try to get something out of life.

2. We must keep our bodies under, so as not to become the slaves of greed.

3. Self-indulgence creeps upon us uncon-

sciously, and must be fought to the bitter end.

A minister once received in his pulpit the following request for prayer:

"The prayers of this congregation are earnestly requested for a man who is prospering in his worldly concerns."

Keep an eye on yourselves, dear children, when you find yourselves looking out for places where your "bread shall be fat," places which, like this land of Asher, will yield you "royal dainties."

IX.

THE BLESSING ON NAPHTALI; or, "THE LIGHT-MINDED SON."

"Naphtali is a hind let loose; he giveth goodly words."—GENESIS xlix. 21.

IF you have ever seen a heifer in a pasture, or a lot of young lambs gamboling about in a meadow, you will know what is meant by a "hind let loose." These young creatures seem to have no law or motive or principle about living. They will crop a little clover, twist their tails, jump and prance around their sedate old parents, and then go through the same pranks again. Indeed, these young creatures behave as if they had the St. Vitus' dance, and could never keep quiet.

When we say of them that they are like

"hinds let loose," we describe them exactly. A hind let loose is the very embodiment of all that is light and foolish and without sense or reason.

Heifers and lambs, kids and colts, calves and kittens, are all undeveloped animals. They are young, and foolish, and immature. They do not know what life is. They think that they are forever to stay in the beautiful green meadows, where there is nothing but clover and mint and running brooks.

Ah! little do they know of the terrible union of mint with spring lamb—or that the clover field is to fit them for the butcher's stall or the hard yoke of service.

What life really is to them they will learn by-and-by, but at present they do not know anything about it; how can they? They are only "hinds let loose" in the pasture field. Jacob said of this son Naphtali that he "was a hind let loose," and then he added, "he giveth goodly words." It is hard to know just what he meant by this. The tribe of Naphtali was situated to the north of Palestine, and its borders were on the waters of the Lake of Gennesareth. The river Jordan flowed by its eastern boundary, and it was a fruitful and populous country. But the tribe of Naphtali was never distinguished for anything in particular. It never seemed to grow into greatness or to develop into any kind of strength.

Perhaps this was because the children of Naphtali—like their father, the head of the tribe—never got beyond the period of the hind in the pasture field.

Some people have the power of growing; some people have the capacity of development in their make-up. Other people stay where they happen to be and never grow at all. They are like calves and lambs and colts which never grow into oxen or sheep or horses.

Our subject to-day is, "Naphtali, the undeveloped or light-minded son."

We learn three lessons from the blessing on "Naphtali."

I.

First. Light-minded persons are very fond of words.

Words are very much like the spring blossoms. They stand for something which is to come after them, and if the fruit never appears the blossoms are of very little worth.

Words are only blossoms. They are the promise of fruit which is to come afterwards, but if the deeds never appear after our words have been uttered, our lives are like the apple-tree which has beautiful blossoms in spring but never has any fruit in October. Now words are very nice things in themselves. "Kind words can never die," the little song says, yet words without thought or action are vain. Jesus Christ our Master did not save the world by the beautiful words which he uttered, but by the deeds which he accomplished. He uttered beautiful words in the Sermon on the Mount, but it was what he did for the world upon Mount Calvary which saved the world.

Look at Job's friends, and at the little they did for him in his hour of trouble. They came and sat down by his side and began to talk to him. Words, words, words, were all that Zophar the Naamathite, and Eliphaz the Temanite, and Bildad the Shuhite offered to poor Job in his troubles. At last he got angry with them for giving him only goodly words in his hour of trouble, and he lifted up his voice and said, "Miserable comforters are ye all." Light-minded, talkative people, who have plenty of words and nothing else, are pretty poor company after all, for we soon grow tired of their endless talk.

Remember this, my dear children, *words are only blossoms, and blossoms are only the promise of fruit,—they are not the fruit itself.*

II.

Secondly. Light-minded persons do not stand the test of time.

It is a great thing in life to learn how to wear well. Some clothes wear well; other articles of clothing wear out easily. Some people and some friendships wear well; other people and other friendships soon wear out. Some friendships need to be kept in perpetual repair. They are all the time going wrong or are getting out of repair, like a cheap three-dollar Waterbury Watch.

I knew a very bright young artist, once, whose pictures were refused at the public exhibition. He was very much surprised. He was dumbfounded, and could not take it in. He had always painted well, from the time when he was a very little boy. His whole life as a boy had been full of promise. He had painted well and painted easily. He had had a boyhood filled with blossoms, and now at the last he had been disappointed. But the trouble was, he had not been wearing well. He had been presuming on his early powers, and had not been careful enough to study up the details of his art. And then he said to his friend: "Now, I'm going to begin to work just as if I had never done anything at all before. I am going to get down to the bottom of things, and start all over again."

That boy was avoiding the mistake of Naphtali,—and will no doubt make a success of his art and become a great painter, simply because he was not content with "blossoms" in the place of fruit; he was not satisfied with mere "goodly words."

There is one character in Pilgrim's Progress who always makes me think of this easy-going Naphtali.

It is the character of Talkative! He was a man who could talk about religion,—and deal out the goodly words of piety!

Hopeful thought there never was such a pilgrim going to the Celestial City as this Talkative, but Christian soon showed his companion that Talkative was a mere Naphtali, only a hind let loose on the journey, whose whole stock in trade of religion consisted in giving forth a set of goodly words.

III.

Thirdly. Light-minded persons should seek for reserve strength.

I have often watched the carpenters and

ship-builders at work in a ship-yard. They have all sorts of material by their side. Some planks are cut out of the heaviest kind of lumber; other planks are made out of the lightest kind of timber. The heavy logs with their great thick-ribbed sides are hewn and cut and fitted into the ship's ribs. These logs are to stand the great storms of the ocean, the ice, the waves, and the rough knocks of the outside world. The light, thin planks, on the other hand, are made into the doors and shutters and woodwork of the cabin. The heavy lumber is not wanted on deck, and the light timber is not wanted on the ship's outside. There is no reserve strength in the timber. When it breaks, it snaps and goes to pieces. But there is a reserve power about the lumber. When it gets a blow from the waves or a knock from the ice, it resists it. It has a strength of its own which is not seen upon the surface. It has a hidden power of its own, and resistance lies dormant in that power.

And this which is true of the character of the wood is true of us. We may be timber or we may be lumber. We may be mere planks for the surface of life, or we may be logs for the realities of life. Light-minded, talkative persons of the Naphtali kind ought to remember that pretty words and phrases are mere blossoms. They are not fruit, and will never become fruit. Actions speak louder than words, or as the old proverb says, "Handsome is that handsome does." Dear children, do not think that you are necessarily good because you talk good or have " good words" about you all the time. Seek continually for "reserve strength," that strength which is the ship's heavy lumber, which will keep it still headed on in the day of stress and storm. Our Lord says to us, as He said to His Apostle of old, " My strength is sufficient for thee." If we have this strength of God in our hearts, we can never make shipwreck of ourselves and fail.

Remember, then, these lessons which we

learn from the blessing upon Naphtali, the undeveloped or light-minded son.

First. Light-minded persons are very fond of words.

Secondly. Light-minded persons do not stand the test of time.

Thirdly. Light-minded persons should seek for reserve strength.

David says in one of his psalms, "I believe, therefore have I spoken." Let us learn not to speak until we believe something deeply and have got something definite to say.

Let us beware of following this easy-go-lucky, hap-hazard, thoughtless kind of life, which we see this son of Jacob possessed.

Let us each try for a better blessing than that which the old patriarch pronounced upon this talkative, easy-going, undeveloped,

NAPHTALI, "THE LIGHT-MINDED SON."

X.

THE BLESSING OF JOSEPH; or "THE FRUITFUL SON."

"Joseph is a fruitful bough, even a fruitful bough by a well; whose branches run over the wall."—GENESIS xlix. 22.

IT is not hard to know a good coin from a bad one. The good coin always has *a true ring to it*. And a good character always has a true ring to it. A true, upright, honest soul can always be detected by the life which is revealed, and not only by the words which are spoken.

There was a good deal of counterfeit coin among the sons of Jacob. These brethren of Joseph were a very poor set. For the most part it was an extremely difficult matter to find anything good in these boys to bless. Their dying father found it a hard matter to say anything very good about them.

But when Jacob came to bless Joseph, the spirit of the old man revived, and he burst forth into a chorus of praise as he thought of all that had happened in the romantic life of his darling son. And so he uttered these words: "Joseph is a fruitful bough, even a fruitful bough by a well; whose branches run over the wall: the archers have sorely grieved him, and shot at him, and hated him: but his bow abode in strength, and the arms of his hands were made strong by the hands of the mighty God of Jacob: (from thence is the shepherd, the stone of Israel). The blessings of thy father have prevailed above the blessings of my progenitors, unto the utmost bound of the everlasting hills; they shall be on the head of Joseph, and on the crown of the head of him that was separate from his brethren." There is no story in all the Bible that is so full of interest to us as the story of Joseph. His beautiful childhood, his cruel treatment by his brothers, his slavery in Egypt, his resistance to temptation, his rise and ascent to power

THE FRUITFUL SON. 143

under Pharaoh, his generosity to his brethren, and his filial devotedness to his father and his family make his life and character famous in the annals of Bible-story.

And yet there was no tribe of Joseph in the promised land, as there was no tribe of Levi. Levi the cruel son and Joseph the fruitful son each drop out of the land of promise. Neither have any inheritance named after them.

But then this is after all a greater honor to Joseph, because the two sons of Joseph, Ephraim and Manasseh, took the place of their father and their uncle Levi. The portion of Manasseh was on the eastern side of the river Jordan and the lake of Galilee, while the tribe of Ephraim was situated on the western side, and became one of the most powerful tribes in Israel.

Ephraim became in time the capital of the ten tribes in the days of the great rebellion, and afterwards was known as the region of Samaria.

I want to speak to you to-day about the blessing of Jacob upon

"THE FRUITFUL SON."

We learn three lessons from this subject.

I.

First.—A fruitful character is the highest kind of man.

What we want in any life is, after all, what we want in a tree or plant. We do not want mere pretty blossoms in Spring: we want fruit in the Fall-time. Pretty words, pretty sayings, pretty manners are all very good in their way; but what God wants of us all, my dear children, and what the world wants of us, is that our lives should have fruit in them, not merely blossoms.

"Joseph is a fruitful bough," said the old patriarch of his darling son. There was not much fruit found among the other children of the family. They seemed like scrubby apple trees at the end of the long row in the orchard. You know how sometimes there will be one or two fine rich trees in an orchard, and then, how all the others will be poor, thin, weak, and scrawny trees, tapering down to some poor little thin one. Well, in this same way Joseph was the strong, rich, fruitful son; the others were, for the most part, the scrub trees of the family orchard.

Now, my dear children, there is a great temptation to us all to-day—in the ease and luxury which is about us, to humor and pet ourselves, and not to make any very great exertion to bring forth fruit in our lives.

If we are easy with ourselves, and do not learn to discipline ourselves, we will never have fruitful lives or become fruitful characters. The gardeners cut and trim and prune the leaves and branches of their trees and vines on purpose to keep from being too luxurious. A fruitful tree or a fruitful bush means one which has been disciplined and pruned, and has been trimmed of its superfluous leaves and branches. And a fruitful life is one which has been treated in exactly the same way.

Joseph had been tempted and tried, and had gone through very heavy sorrows. And the result of it all was that when he came to the throne of Pharaoh he was a rich, strong, noble character, and his life was a faithful one. But the other boys of Jacob—the brethren of Joseph—did not have their characters pruned and tried, and the result was that they were not faithful in their lives.

No life, my dear children, can be successful if there is no fruit about it.

It is not the man who can talk well, or the man who can dress well, or the man who is rich, or learned, or powerful, who is the fruitful or successful man. It is the man whose life tells what he is, and who by his deeds fulfils our Lord's words when He said, "By their fruits ye shall know them."

There was a wonderful picture in New York in the late Morgan collection, which has made a great effect by the power there is in it. It is called, "The Story of the Missionary." An old monk, with blows and bruises over his head and arms, is reciting the story of his adventures in the mission-field to a group of cardinals and church dignitaries in Rome. One is playing with a dog; another is sipping his coffee; a third is pouring out a glass of wine, and is laughing; a fourth is looking through his glasses at the missionary, as if he did not believe his story could be possible; a fifth is listening to a funny story which a companion is whispering in his ear, and a sixth, with his hand upon his forehead, is drinking in the words of the enraptured monk, as with closed eyes he goes over the recital of his doings for the love of Jesus Christ.

It is a wonderful picture. The whole meaning of life is there. It is not hard to tell which is the fruitful life. It is not the life which has power, or luxury, or the good things of this world about it. It is the life which is fruitful in results which is the truely successful life.

II.

Secondly.—A fruitful character always has some secret source of supply.

"Joseph is a fruitful bough, even a bough by a well." A bough by a well is one which draws up its supplies by its roots from the water which is near it. Willow-trees in the first touch of Spring-time, seem to be greener than any of the other trees about them. The pussy willows seem to be the first of all the green things which open at the touch of Spring. But the real reason why they bloom before the other trees is that they grow near the running brooks, so that their roots run deep down and suck in their full supply of water.

Or perhaps you may sometime have watched how the hyacinth bulbs in glass jars have sent down their long white roots into the water, and have taken all their growth and sustenance from it. They are beautiful and fruitful plants, because their roots go down into the water and get their strength from it.

And Jacob said of his darling son Joseph that he was a fruitful bough—"even a bough by a well." In other words, he had some secret source of supply from which he drew his strength.

Joseph's well, or the source of his supply and strength of character, was his faith in God. He knew that God would not desert him. He knew that however dark his life might look there was a divine eye watching over him, and a divine hand leading him. This faith in God kept him firm in the hour of temptation, patient in the hour of suffering, and calm and undisturbed in the hour of success and triumph.

We all have our "wells" in life from which we draw our supply of strength. Perhaps it may be our mother, or some Sunday-school teacher or friend, or some church or good book, or some minister who always helps us to be brave and true and good. Perhaps if we try we can be "wells" to one another, and can help instead of hindering one another on the journey of life. Some people discourage and hinder us; other people help us and cheer us by their kindness and their courage. Some friendships are discouraging; other friendships are full of help and assistance. Many a man draws his supply of strength in life from some brave, true wife. Many a man's well of strength to which his roots go down for nourishment is his faith in God, which perhaps has been taught him by his mother.

God said to Abraham on one occasion, "Fear not, Abraham, I am thy shield and thy exceeding great reward."

It is a great thing to get behind the fact of God as our helper and defender.

This was what made Luther and Washington and Lincoln so strong. They were "boughs by a well." The roots of their nature went down into the deep ground where the springs are. And they were strong because their sources of supply were strong.

Remember this lesson of our subject, my dear children: a fruitful character always has some secret source of supply.

III.

Thirdly.—A fruitful character always outgrows its boundaries.

THE FRUITFUL SON. 151

"Whose branches run over a wall."

I have seen tomato plants and "dusty miller" and "morning glories" spread all over their own separate little patch in the garden, and throw themselves wherever they could find an inch of earth to grow in.

There is no such thing as keeping some kind of plants in their narrow little garden beds. If they are to grow at all they must grow "over the wall."

And there is no such thing as keeping certain people within narrow bounds. If a man is not too large for his place he is generally too small for it. Joseph was one of those persons who always grow over the wall of their surroundings. When he was a boy in Goshen he grew over into his father's life and cared for him. When he was a prisoner in Egypt, he grew over the wall which separated him from his companions in prison and cared for the butler and the baker. When he was a prince upon the throne he grew over the wall and cared for all the people of Egypt, and for his own family who were starving in Canaan. All through his eventful life Jacob's description of Joseph was true: "Joseph is a fruitful bough, even a fruitful bough by a well; whose branches grow over the wall."

We can all remember in the country how some generous-minded apple tree or some kind-hearted cherry tree let their richly freighted branches grow over the wall for the passers-by to gather their fruit. They do not seem to be willing to keep all their fruit for themselves. They let their branches bend over the wall for others.

And so it is of us. If we have fruit in our lives we must be willing to let it run over the wall of our boundaries for the sake of others.

Now, my dear children, we must not keep our lives fenced in to our own little enclosure, like some thin little sapling shut in by its own tree-box. We must grow out of our own home-life, and our set of friends, and our own way of looking at things. For the trees which do not grow over the wall are most generally the trees which have very little fruit upon them.

These then are the lessons which we learn from the blessing of Jacob upon his son Joseph.

1st. A fruitful character is the highest kind of man.

2d. A fruitful character always has some secret source of supply.

3d. A fruitful character always outgrows its surroundings.

There is one thing very singular about this blessing upon Joseph. We do not know when or where the other sons of Jacob died or what became of their bones.

But the bones of Joseph were carried up with the children of Israel when they went up out of Egypt into Canaan. We are told they embalmed Joseph in Egypt.

Here is the closing thought for us. If we are fruitful in our lives we shall be embalmed in the memory of our friends, and they will always carry with them the remains of our fruitful lives.

XI.

THE BLESSING ON BENJAMIN; or, "THE SON OF THE RIGHT HAND."

"Benjamin shall ravin as a wolf; in the morning he shall devour the prey, and at night he shall divide the spoil."—GENESIS xlix. 27.

THERE is a period in almost everybody's life, when he feels that he must go to sea. Most bad boys, and some good ones have gone to sea, or have been stowaways on some ship or emigrant train.

It is a part of our nature, when we are young, to want to roam. We want to travel and wander away out of sight and sound of our home duties and home companions. Those words of our text to-day sound just like the wild pirate we have often wished we could become when we were boys at school. "Benjamin shall ravin as a wolf: in the morn.

ing he shall devour the prey, and at night he shall divide the spoil."

The tribe of Benjamin was one of the most interesting and powerful of all the tribes in the Holy Land. "There is little Benjamin, their ruler," this is the way in which this tribe is spoken of in one of the psalms. The great capital of all the tribes, Jerusalem, was in its borders. The boundary between Judah and Benjamin ran at the foot of the hill on which the city stands, so that the city of Jerusalem itself was actually in Benjamin, while by crossing the narrow ravine of Hinnom, one could set foot on the territory of Judah. The River Jordan ran by the side of the territory of Benjamin, and the Dead Sea was below it.

All the modern Jews have come from the two tribes of Judah and Benjamin. These two tribes formed the kingdom of Judah. The other ten tribes formed the kingdom of Israel. The ten tribes were carried away captive into Syria, and we do not know what became of them or their descendants.

All the Jews who are in Europe and America have descended from the two tribes of Judah and Benjamin.

But to come back again to the blessing of Jacob upon Benjamin. We shall find that this Benjamin was a very different character in after life, from that which he was in his younger days. In the morning of his days, he wanted to devour the prey: at night he wanted to divide the spoil.

That is, in his early days he wanted everything that he could lay his hands on *for himself*: in after life he was ready and willing to divide what he had with others. This is what is meant by devouring the prey, and then dividing the spoil.

In other words, Benjamin was a changed or converted character in his manhood, from that which he was in his boyhood. He made a change of base in his life—from looking out always for No. 1, to looking out for others. Instead of devouring everything himself, he learned how to divide his good things with others.

We read in the Bible that when Rachel, his mother, lay dying, after the birth of Benjamin, that she called his name Benoni, but that his father called him Benjamin. Benoni means son of sorrow—a son of the left hand; while the word Benjamin means a son of comfort—a son of the right hand.

One of the most interesting and instructive sermons I ever remember as a boy, was a sermon by my father, at old St. Paul's Church, in Philadelphia, at the Children's Church Service there, on the subject of "The Marks of a Benoni." You will find it in the "Rills from the Fountain of Life," and I advise you to get it and read it for yourselves.

Benjamin then was first of all a Benoni. He was a left-handed son, a son of sorrow. But after a while he changed his base and became a Benjamin—a son of blessing—a right-handed son.

And here I think we find our subject to-day, about

"Benjamin the Left-handed, and Benjamin the Right-handed Son."

You know how awkward it is to be left-handed,—to write with one's left hand, and to work with one's left hand, and to eat with one's left hand.

Now there are boys and girls in every family who are left-handed in their character. They do their duties in an awkward, miserable, bungling way. They keep sprawling over their morals, and make sad work of their every-day duties.

All they think of is—that which Benjamin thought of when he was young, viz.—how they can devour their prey, and get a good share of things for themselves.

Now, how can left-handed sons become right-handed sons? How can we change our idea of life from the thought of devouring the prey, to the thought of dividing the spoil? How can we change our name from Benoni, the Son of Sorrow, to Benjamin, the Son of Blessing?

Well, in order to do this, we must follow the steps which Benjamin took in his life.

I.

First.—We must remember that always looking out for self does not bring a blessing.

A ravening wolf on the mountain side is not a very agreeable companion. The wolves which come out after travellers, as they drive in their sleighs through the snow-fields of Russia, are not pleasant or agreeable creatures to meet.

A ravening wolf is hungry, and hunger makes him cruel, so that all a wolf ever thinks of is the matter of devouring the prey. A wolf is never ready or willing to divide the spoil.

I can remember at the old Episcopal Academy in Philadelphia, when Doctor Hare was the principal, and Mr. Bushbeck and Mr. Edwards were the teachers there, how the boys who played marbles down in the play-yard, would call out : " Me first ! Me first !" That is, each boy wanted the first shot at the pile of marbles. He wanted to devour the prey before the other boys would ever have a chance.

"Me first." Ah! my dear children, how we carry this motto with us all through life. We want to be first at home; first in business; first in church matters; first in receiving honors and compliments, and first in everything which will be for our own interests. But this habit of always looking out for our own little pet-selves will not make us happy. God made us to live for him and not for others, and if we only live for ourselves, and grow to be selfish and greedy, we will starve a part of our nature, which was made for God, and which never can be happy till it finds God.

As I walk the streets of our great cities, and see the crowds of people there, I do not find many noble-looking faces. People are in a hurry; people look fat and coarse; people seem as if they were looking out for themselves, as the wolf does, when he is on the scent of his prey. There is a great deal of unhappiness in the world to-day, and the principle cause of it all is found in the fact that this is a commercial age. People are all the time thinking of buying and selling, and of what they can get and of what they can make. There are a great many Benonis in the world to-day; left-handed people, who do not realize that always looking out for one's self does not bring a blessing.

Why, I have learnt this very lesson from three of my dogs. Let me tell you about them. One is a pug and is named Spunk; the other two dogs are Skye-terriers, and are named Dottie and Pettie. Well, every night after supper, last winter, these dogs got into the way of whining for crackers. There was no such a thing as stopping them. They would sit up on their hind legs and whine, and whine, and finally they would break out into a howl. They used to call out something which sounded like "Hello," at a telephone office.

Well, in order to stop all this noise I got them each a wooden bowl, and broke up plenty of crackers in them. I would put in enough crackers to last for a whole evening, more than they could possibly eat. And what do you suppose happened? Why, these miserable—selfish, Benoni—left-handed dogs, would spend the whole evening, each one with his head in his own bowl, not because he wanted any more crackers, but because each dog was afraid the other dog would be after his bowl. So after awhile they were cured of wanting more crackers, because the responsibility of looking after their bowl was too great for them.

Many a time as I have heard them growl over their bowls, too full to eat any more, but too selfish to leave their treasure, I have thought: "Oh, you dogs, how much you are like the people in the world of to-day."

"In the morning he shall devour the prey."

This was the mark of Benoni—the left-handed son of Jacob.

The first subject of our lesson to-day is: that always looking after self does not bring a blessing.

II.

Secondly.—We must remember that sharing our good things with others, is God's way of being made happy.

I was reading the other day about what a little peasant boy did for his father in the Prussian army.

The story is as follows:

During the year 1790, as the French and Prussian armies stood face to face, a little boy, whose father stood in the Prussian ranks, happened to hear that the provisions for the army were ill-supplied, and that even money was unable to buy food.

The constant repetition of this sank deeply into the little fellow's mind, and as he knew his mother had plenty of potatoes he determined to carry some to his father.

So anxious was he to set off, that he could not wait for his mother's return from the neighboring village, but filled a sack with potatoes and started away towards the Rhine, for he knew that his father's regiment lay encamped at Mainz, and he had learnt the shortest way thither from the schoolmaster.

Every place he arrived at with his burden the people willingly gave him food and shelter; and an empty cart, going the direction of Mainz, lightened his labor and brought him safely into the Prussian camp.

When he had made known his business and his father's name, the captain of the latter's company ordered the lad with his sack into his tent, and sent for his father. The joy of both was indeed great, and the happy father kept the little fellow in camp until he had recovered from the effects of his long journey.

The captain and other officers, who took an uncommon liking for the plucky little traveller, rewarded him handsomely; as did the French, too, into whose hands he afterwards fell, for they treated him kindly; and their general, Custine, even made him a present and set him free again.

This little fellow was a true Benjamin. He was a right-handed son. He was not thinking all the time of how he was to "devour the prey." He was thinking how he might be able in some way to divide his good things with others.

My dear children, when we have got the wolf and dog out of us; I mean by this, when we no longer think all the time of how we can devour the prey; when we think of others and share our good things with them, by kind words and deeds, then we are no longer Benonis' or left-handed children; we are Benjamins': children of the right hand.

Benjamin began in the wrong way, but he came out all right at the last. In the morning he devoured the prey, but at night he divided the spoil. Benjamin began life as a Benoni; a son of trouble, a "left-handed" son in the family, but he crossed over at last to the side of the "right-handed" children of the household, and ended by being a son of comfort.

Remember these two lessons of our sermon to-day.

1st. Always looking out for self does not bring a blessing.

2d. Sharing our good things with others is God's way of being happy.

Now, then, all you Benonis, you left-handed boys and girls, get over to the Benjamin side of life, the right-handed side, as quickly as you can.

You cannot make this change of base but with God's special grace helping you.

Therefore, pray to the Lord Jesus Christ every day for his divine help, to make you children of comfort to all about you.

XII.

O. P. J.,
or, THE FATHER HIMSELF WHO BLESSED HIS BOYS.

"And when Jacob had made an end of commanding his sons, he gathered up his feet into the bed, and yielded up the ghost, and was gathered unto his people."
—GENESIS xlix. 33.

I WANT in the closing Sermon of this course, on "An Old Man's Blessing," to speak about the father himself who blessed his boys. The old patriarch Jacob.

But perhaps you wonder why I have put the letters "O. P. J." to this twelfth Sermon?

Let me tell you a story. Some years ago there was a broker on Third Street, Philadelphia, who had a large office, and did a large business.

There were a number of young men in the

outer office, whom this broker would frequently call into his inner office and would say, "put down $25," or "put down $50 to the O. P. J. account." Nobody knew what these mysterious letters "O. P. J." meant.

Some thought they meant "old public journalists." Others thought they meant "Junior Order of Presbyterians," while still others thought they stood for "Junkets Odd and Proper." But no one could find out what this mysterious account meant, until at last it was discovered that the letters O. P. J. stood for the "Old Patriarch Jacob."

You see the old patriarch Jacob gave one-tenth of all his income to the Lord, according to a vow which he had made on the night when he lay down to sleep in the wilderness and saw the vision of the angels of God ascending upon the ladder to Heaven.

At that time he promised that if the Lord would take care of him and bring him back again to his father's house in peace, he would surely give to the Lord one-tenth of all that he acquired.

A Father who Blessed His Boys. 171

It was from this vow of Jacob's that the Jewish custom of the tithe or tenth part arose.

The Jewish tithes were the tenth part of the earnings of the people, and this custom of giving the tithes arose from the vow of Jacob, the father of the Jewish people, on the night when he went forth from his father's house, and had the vision of Heaven opened.

So then the "O. P. J." account of this banker on Third Street in Philadelphia was his "Lord's Treasury" account, or his charity fund. And whenever he gave anything to the Lord's cause he used to say "put it down to the O. P. J. account."

Perhaps you would like to have me tell you the name of this person. But as this is a sermon and not a story, I must stop the story and go on with the sermon; and it is not proper, you know, to call out people's names in sermons.

The old patriarch Jacob then—who had been through so many changes and had so many strange experiences in life—was dying.

He had blessed all his children as they knelt by his bed-side, and now that he had finished his words and had made an end of blessing his sons, we read that he "gathered up his feet into the bed and yielded up the ghost, and was gathered unto his people."

He was tired of all the strife and confusion of life.

He was an old man—and the one thing left to an old man to do in life is to bless his household before he dies.

I was reading the other day some lines written by an old man who was tired of having to live. They are as follows:

"I am tired. Heart and feet
Turn from the busy mart and street;
I am tired—rest is sweet.

I am tired. I have played
In the sunshine and the shade,
I have seen the flowers fade.

I am tired. I have had
What has made my spirit glad,
What has made my spirit sad.

A Father who Blessed His Boys.

> I am tired. Loss and gain!
> Golden sheaves and scattered grain!
> Day has not been spent in vain.
>
> I am tired. Eventide
> Bids me lay my cross aside,
> Bids me in my hopes abide.
>
> I am tired. God is near,
> Let me sleep without a fear,
> Let me die without a tear.
>
> I am tired. I would rest
> As the bird within its nest;
> I am tired. Home is best."

Now it must have seemed very strange to the old patriarch Jacob to look back upon his past life and try to make it all out. It will seem very strange to us at last when we come to die, to look back upon our life.

As Jacob on his dying bed looked back upon his life, he saw that his life was made up of three things.

And the life of each one of us is made up of these same three things.

I.

First there is what we have, or what is called *heredity.*

By heredity or inheritance we mean what we have coming down to us by descent from our forefathers.

The cat inherits her sense of prowling after her prey at night. The terrier dog inherits his sense of scent: the Newfoundland dog and the water spaniel inherit their love of the water from their ancestors.

The different kinds of horses inherit their own special traits from their forefathers, as the race horse, the cart horse, and the carriage horse.

They are what they are because there is something in the blood which goes to make them what they are.

And, my dear children—we have all got something within us which has come down to us from our fathers. We are like vessels with a heavy cargo inside. We may have passion, anger, pride, jealousy, revenge, greed, selfishness, cruelty, and deceit wrapped up in our natures, as these sons of Jacob had, and by-and-bye when we get out into some of the hard places of life, something will give a lunge or set to our nature in that direction—and it will become very evident that we have got something on our deck or stowed away within, which has come down to us from our fathers. Depend upon it the first thing which goes to make up our life is—*what we have.*

II.

The second thing which goes to make up our life is *what we are,* or, *habit.*

It is hard for us ourselves, to know just what we are. We do not see ourselves as others see us. St. James says in one place that we behold our natural face in the glass and go our way and forget what manner of person we are. Now we are all drifting somewhere. We are either drifting into good habits or into bad habits. We are either getting better or getting worse. None of us are standing still.

Why even the icebergs, which seem to be great islands, are all floating to the south. Nothing in nature stands still. The seasons run into one another; the rivers run to the sea; the great mountains crumble away. And we are all drifting somewhere and into some kind of life. Our habits are becoming fixed upon us all the time, and, sooner or later, will make us their captives. We ought to look into our hearts every little while; we ought to take an inventory of our nature as the storekeepers take an account of stock every new year—just to see what we have upon our shelves.

Old George Herbert says in one of his quaint poems:

"By all means use some time to be alone:
  Salute thyself: see what thy soul doth wear.
  Dare to look in thy box, for 'tis thine own,
  And tumble up and down what thou find'st there."

The second thing which goes to make up life is *what we are—or habit.*

III.

The third thing which goes to make up our life is *what we have made ourselves, or character*.

To make one's own fortune is a great deal better after all than to inherit it or to drift into it. A thing which we have made for ourselves, is generally better and more valuable to us than a thing which has been given to us or which we have stumbled upon by accident.

To conquer ourselves and earn a character by a resolute and determined act of the will is better for us after all, than to be merely innocent, or to be good because some one stands over us and makes us good. To earn a character is better than to inherit a character or to drift into goodness of living, just as to earn a fortune makes us stronger men and women than to inherit one, or to stumble upon one by accident.

As the old patriarch Jacob looked back upon his life from his dying bed, he must have seen that it was made up of these three things: inheritance, and habit, and character. And he must have thanked God that he was what he was, not because he had inherited his character from his father or had drifted into it by accident, but that by the help of God he had won it for himself through the struggles of his life.

As he looked back over his life, he must have seen that it was, after all, that struggle with himself which he had when he wrestled by the brook Jabbok and changed his name from Jacob the supplanter to Israel, a prince having power and prevailing with God—which made him the strong man he was when he came to die.

Jacob's career teaches us that life is made up of these three things.

1st. What we have, or, *heredity.*

2d. What we are, or *habit.*

3d. What we may become, or *character.*

And now we are through with these twelve sermons on the blessing of the sons of Jacob.

I hope my dear young friends that you

will not forget the lessons which we have learned from these far off children of the old patriarch.

If you make your life a blessing to those about you, those about you will give you their blessing in return.

Will you not offer this short prayer? "Oh Lord Jesus Christ, give me thy blessing, that my life may be a blessing to others, as thou hast lived and died to bless this sinning world!" *Amen.*

XIII.

"REALIZED DREAMS."

"I the Lord * * will speak unto him in a dream."
NUMBERS xii. 6.

THIS is a wheelbarrow sermon. Perhaps you never heard of a "wheelbarrow sermon" before. Well, I will tell what I mean by a wheelbarrow sermon. A wheelbarrow is something which runs upon one wheel and is pushed by two handles. The wheel is the thing on which the barrow runs, but there must also be a man to take up the two handles of the barrow and push the load along.

So I propose to push this sermon home from behind, but I want the sermon to move upon a story. So as the story is the wheel and the lessons are the load, and I am the minister pushing the load from behind, I have called this sermon about "Realized Dreams" a wheelbarrow sermon.

These words which I have taken for our text to-day tell us that the Lord said to Moses, "If there be a prophet among you, *I* the Lord will make myself known unto him in a vision, and will speak unto him in a dream."

It is very strange that sometimes our best and purest desires and intentions come to us with our opening thoughts, as if some of God's angels had visited us in the night and had given us those holy thoughts of Him. And what God was able to do in olden times, to His servants and prophets, He is able to do to His children to-day. So for one I believe in this way God has of speaking to His children in their dreams. And so I have called this sermon, "Realized Dreams."

The story *will* come first, for it is the story which makes the sermon go, and then the lessons will come afterwards. Now for the story.

In the Cummington churchyard, far up among the Berkshire Hills, in Massachusetts, is a church which is called "Cudnor Church."

You will not find this church on the map by its name, or in the Diocesan report, but nevertheless there it stands.

There was a little girl in this church, whose name was Elsie, and on a certain Christmas Eve she was in the church along with the others dressing the church for the services on Christmas day. Elsie had a hard time of it with her relations, because they did not believe as she believed. Her uncle John and brother Tom and aunt Cora used to make a great deal of fun at Elsie's expense. Well, as I was saying, on this Christmas Eve they were all in the church helping to deck it with evergreens and boughs and hollyberries. Elsie's uncle John had been having a good laugh over a mistake Elsie had made when she was a little girl. Her uncle John had asked Elsie what a missionary was, after one of the missionary meetings which had been held in the church, and Elsie had replied that they lived in the water and ate up little heathen children. But Elsie was only four years old when she made this mistake of calling crocodiles, missionaries.

Her brother Tom, too, had a great deal of fun at Elsie's expense, because she had said that a friend of hers at school had a brother at a boarding-school in Maine, where, he said, they had "bears and religious privileges" in their country. But this was not all. Elsie's aunt Cora, who was president of the Bishop Seabury Prayer-Book Society, did not believe in foreign missions, and she thought Elsie was very foolish to want to give the money of the church to missions, when they needed a new carpet in the church and a set of white hangings for Christmas and Easter.

But Elsie's Sunday-school class had four quarterly collections a year, and the money of this class was given to four little heathen children.

First there was little Sing Paw, a Chinese

girl in Shanghai, then there was Grebo Dick, an African boy at the Cape Mount school at Cape Palmas, in Africa. Hans Littleman was an Esquimau boy. He was the third heathen child Elsie and her fellow scholars helped along. They had heard of him through a speech which Archdeacon Kirkby had made in their church, and they resolved to give one-fourth of their annual collection to this little fellow.

Ben Hassan was their fourth heathen ward. He was an Arab boy, in Dr. Jessup's school in Beirut, Syria. He had the remaining fourth of Elsie's collections.

Not content, however, with giving money to these children, and then thinking no more about them, little Elsie had secured their photographs, and had them each framed and hung up on the wall by the old square pew where her class and their teacher sat.

So it came to pass that on this particular Christmas Eve, while uncle John and brother Tom, and aunt Cora had been trimming up the church for the services on Christmas day, little Elsie had been putting a wreath around each of these four pictures of their little heathen wards.

But
  there was one thing
    Elsie could not
      understand.
She could not understand how all of a sudden she had followed the crowd, and had gone into a garden. There was ever so much light all around, and when she asked the people what it all meant, they replied that they were all going to meet the Lord Jesus Christ in Paradise, and that this was the way to get there. Presently she met little Sing Paw from China; she knew her by the picture; and then she saw Grebo Dick; he was running in to meet the Lord Jesus Christ; and Hans Littleman was hurrying in along with the others, and Ben Hassan was waving his red Turkish fez cap with a black tassel to it. They were all hurrying along with the others into the light of the beautiful garden. Elsie could not

make it out. "Oh, I'm so glad we helped Sing Paw and Grebo Dick and Hans Littleman and Ben Hassan," cried Elsie, "but, dear me; oh, where am I?"

* * * * *

"You've been asleep, Elsie, dear," replied her aunt Cora. "You fell asleep on the pile of greens as you were putting wreaths around those absurd pictures of the little heathen children. Do you ever expect to meet them in heaven, Elsie?"

"I have met them already, aunt Cora," replied Elsie. "I have just parted from them this very minute. I have seen them this very night in my dream. Some day I will see them with my own eyes."

Now then, this story is the *wheel* upon which the rest of the sermon is to run, this sermon which I have called my wheelbarrow sermon.

Now comes the pushing part.

If we want to realize our dreams in the Christian life, we must all have three rules in our life.

I.

First of all, *we must have the rule of praying*. This is the first rule in our Christian rule of three. This is the first fact in the Christian life for us. It is the beginning of everything for us. We find that our Lord Jesus Christ, though He was the Son of God, always prayed to His Father in Heaven before He began any great work, or after He had been healing the sick and the miserable. He prayed all night before He chose His disciples to be His companions and followers. And in the first chapter of St. Mark's Gospel we read these words: "And He healed many that were sick of divers diseases, and cast out many devils, and in the morning, rising up a great while before day, He went out, and departed into a solitary place, and *there* prayed." What an example Jesus here sets us of beginning our different duties with prayer. If He was the Son of God, and yet needed to pray to His Father in Heaven before He undertook any great work, how much more should we, who are sinful, while He was sinless, learn to pray to our Heavenly Father before we undertake any hard duty. We ought to think of prayer to God as a petition which we make in a court. We must go about it in the right way. We must know what we want, and then having complied with all the legal requirements, we must leave the matter in the hands of the court. Prayer is nothing more than petitioning God, just as we petition some human court of justice. There is just as much reason in praying to God as there is in petitioning a court to grant us our request. If it is right for us to have what we ask for, and if it is within the range of the court's ruling, we will most probably receive an answer to our petition. And so it is with prayer, which is after all only a petition to God in his own law court.

When the great explorer and missionary, Dr. Livingstone, was found by Stanley's exploring party in mid Africa, he was found dead upon his knees. Dr. Livingstone died praying, and he was not a man, with all his scientific knowledge, to be a believer in superstition. He wanted to do a great work for Africa, and he knew that the first rule of success in the Christian life, the first rule in the Christian rule of three, was "*The rule of praying.*"

II.

The second rule in the Christian rule of three *is the rule of giving.*

We hear a great many people say to-day that God is not real to them. But He is not real to them because they are not real to Him.

The Jews of old time never had any trouble in finding God a real God to them. They gave Him a real place in their lives, and He became as much of a reality to them as a bank becomes a reality to us in which we deposit our money. Anything in which we deposit our money or funds becomes a reality to us. But if we never give anything to God or His cause in the world, or if we think that we must wait until we can say that charity begins at home, then we will never find an unseen God a living reality to us. If you don't give anything for God, and if you have no place for Him in your life, He will never be a reality to you. It is the rule of giving which binds God to you and makes Him a living reality to you.

A lady said to me the other day, " I do wish you would not give out so many notices of appeals for Foreign Missions. I don't believe in Foreign Missions, and never give one cent for them. I think charity begins at home." And all I said to her was this: "Do you think the Saviour of the world died only for *your little set?* I would like to know where you and I would have been if the Church of old had said, we don't believe in Foreign Missions! You and I would have been Druids, offering up our children in sacrifice, if the Church of the past had talked this kind of nonsense which you, a baptized Christian, are talking to-day." We must give to others, as others have given to us. The second rule in the Christian rule of three, is *the rule of giving*.

III.

The third rule in the Christian rule of three is the rule of working.

Praying and giving are each excellent things to bring about our desired ends, but the third rule of Christian success, the rule of working, must crown and supplement the other two rules.

There is a great deal of criticism going on to-day upon all people who try to do anything. The newspapers find fault with people if they try to do anything. Critics write their pieces on every book, or picture, or piece of music, or work of art that comes out, and show the mistakes the people have made who have done the work, and how different it ought to be, and how much better it could be done if others had only taken their advice. All the generals who lost battles in the war of the Rebellion are writing pieces to-day in the magazines, showing the many mistakes of those who were in command, and just how the whole affair ought to have been handled.

Now, criticism is all very good, and we ought never to be above being criticised, only, an hour's honest work ourselves is better than whole days of criticism of others.

Let us learn to do something in this world for the Lord Jesus Christ and for our fellowmen, and not to get into the way of standing off with our eye-glasses and criticising the Lord's hard workers, and saying just how it ought to be done. If we can make a clock go, or a wagon go, or a horse go, or a boy go, or a Sunday-school class or a church go, it is a great deal better after all than having a score of doctors standing by and telling us just how the thing ought to be done. Working is always better than talking. The Lord loveth a cheerful giver. We are never told that He loveth a mere talker, no matter how long or well he may talk.

This then, my dear children, is my wheelbarrow sermon to-day. The story was the wheel, and it came first; the lessons are the barrow and they came afterwards.

Little Elsie in Cudnor Church believed in praying for the heathen, in giving for the heathen, and in working for the heathen.

And she had her dream fulfilled, for she saw Sing Paw, Grebo Dick, Hans Littleman and Ben Hassan in her dream that Christmas Eve night at Cudnor Church, and she knows that she will see them all some day, and that the same Lord who spoke to her once in a dream will speak to her again in reality.

So then, my dear children, if we want to see what we are hoping for come true, let us keep on using these same three rules in the Christian life. I. The rule of praying. II. The rule of giving. III. The rule of working.

And in this way the Lord will answer our prayers and will help us to realize our dreams, which we dream for him.

XIV.

SERMONS FROM THE CLOCK.

"The sun to rule by day."—Psalm cxxxvi. 8.

A CLOCK is a very wonderful thing. Perhaps you have never stopped to think what a wonderful thing it is.

Suppose then to-day that you stop for a few moments while we talk together about some *lessons from the clock*.

We get the idea of time from the sun. We read in the first chapter of the book of Genesis that "God made two great lights; the sun to rule the day, and the moon to rule the night; he made the stars also." And in this 136th Psalm, which was probably written by Ezra, and was sung by the Jews on the occasion of their return to their own land again, when they rebuilt their temple, the praise of the people is given to God, in the oft-repeated refrain of this well-known Psalm, as the priests and Levites sang it antiphonally on either side of the Sanctuary, —"His mercy endureth forever."

And thus they sang these words of our text to-day:—

"To him that made great lights: for his mercy endureth forever:

The sun to rule by day: for his mercy endureth forever:

The moon and stars to rule by night: for his mercy endureth forever."

Now, when we come to think of it, we find that we cannot get on in life without a clock or a watch, or some standard of time.

But the sun is after all the true standard of all time. All our ideas of hours and minutes, and nights and days, and months and years come from the sun and the moon.

The sea captain in mid-ocean finds out what the true time is by taking his observations with the sextant, an instrument which enables him to look at the sun, and find just where the sun is on his maps. Before clocks were invented, King Alfred discovered a way of telling the hours of the day by means of a candle, which burned just so many sections in the course of twenty-four hours.

He placed his hour-candle in a horn lantern, to keep it from being blown out, and this was the way they told the time in the palaces and monasteries of England. Then, long before clocks were invented, people had hour-glasses, such as little girls have nowadays when they practice upon the piano. This is what the old poets mean by "the sands of life" running out.

This is the way the ancients knew what time it was. But after all, the sun-dial, like our modern clock, had the sun for its standard, so that the sun which rules the day is after all the thing from which a clock gets its idea of time.

Every business in the world is run by the standard of time which the clock keeps.

Railroads, steamboats, factories, schools, officers, churches, hotels, all are governed by the clock.

The clock on the mantelpiece, or the old grandfather's clock on the stairs, is the great regulator of our life.

When we take the works of a clock to be mended, how vacant the big round hole seems, where our dear old friend and counsellor used to be! And it has always seemed to me that the person who denies the existence of God takes out of *this* world the face of the world's standard and regulator. Life seems just as meaningless and empty without a belief in God, as the home seems when the face of the clock has been taken away, and there is nothing but a vacant hole in the place where our dear old friend has been.

There was a Welshman once, whose name was James Ap Jones. He used to spend his evenings very frequently at the ale-house, until it was morning. When he came home his wife, who always used to sit up for him, would call out, "James Ap Jones, look at the clock! look at the clock!" This used to wear him out so, that after he went out to the ale-house, he would frequently return and set the clock back, so that it would not be late when he returned. But his wife found out his trick, and used to keep on with her one remark whenever he returned, "Look at the clock, Mr. Jones, look at the clock." The clock was the judge which always condemned him. Now, my dear children, I want you to-day to

"Look at the clock."

We will take the clock all to pieces, and then put it together again, and find out the lessons which it teaches us.

I.

First of all I would say, that the face of a clock is of no use without the hands of a clock. A clock without hands might just as well be a painted clock. Children in the country very often have what they call a "turnip watch." That is, they take a turnip and shave off or pare off one side of it, and then on that open face they paint the hours and the hands of a clock. But that "turnip watch" is of no use whatever, simply because the hands remain in the same position, they do not move round the face of the clock, and therefore do not tell the true time of the day.

It is the hands of a clock which give character to the face of a clock. The hands show whether there is life within the clock or not, and whether or not the clock is going too fast or too slow, or just right. Here is the first lesson which the clock teaches us: It is *the hands which give character to the face.*

What we do with our hands, shows itself in our life, and our face is always the tell-tale of our character. You can nearly always tell what a person is by his face. What he does with his hands shows itself in his face. A painter, a sculptor, a clergyman, a doctor, a lawyer, generally show by their faces what they are.

I saw, not long ago, on a bench in the Pittsfield Jail, a row of criminals.

They had chains and handcuffs on their arms; one man had stolen, another man was a forger, a third had been in a drunken brawl and had shot a companion. But the evil works which they had done showed in the face of each of them. The works of their hands told in their faces.

This then is the first lesson which we learn when we "look at the clock."

The face of a clock is of no use without the hands of a clock.

II.

Secondly, we learn from looking at a clock that the hands of a clock are of no use without the works of a clock.

If the hands of a clock are to go at all, there must always be some works back of the hands to make them go.

When the English first went to China with their steam vessels, the Emperor of China was so much pleased with the appearance of the steamers, that he told his ship builders to instantly make two such ships such as the English had. So the Chinese carpenters went to work and built two or three steamers out of some old Chinese junks, and in order to make the vessels look like the English steamer, they put shavings and sticks on fire down in a big iron cauldron in the vessels' holds, and had the smoke come up through a large red pipe. They were very fine looking ships, and made a great deal more smoke than the English steamers. There was only one trouble with them, however. They wouldn't go, simply because they had no works inside.

The smoke-stacks on those Chinese war steamers were of no use, simply because there were no works with which they were connected.

"Mary," said a Sunday-school teacher one day to her little scholar, "Mary, you say you must resist the works of the devil; what are the works of the devil?"

Mary did not know. She was a little girl, and her father was a clock-maker. She had often seen her father take his clocks and watches to pieces and mend them. So presently she replied, "Please ma'am, I think the devil's works must be what is inside of him, and what he puts into our insides."

The teacher and the children could not help laughing over little Mary's mistake, but her answer was a very good one after all.

It is our good or bad works within us, our good or bad thoughts, desires, and inclinations which make our hands do good or bad deeds, which good or bad deeds show in our face. The second lesson we learn from looking at a clock is this: The hands of a clock are of no use without the works of a clock.

III.

Thirdly we learn from a clock that the works of a clock are of no use without a regulator.

The regulator is that part of a clock's machinery which keeps the works in good running order.

The regulator keeps the clock from going too fast or from going too slow, and in this way makes the hours and minutes of the day correspond to the sun's time in the heavens.

If a clock does not go right it is better that it should not go at all, for then it will at least be right twice a day, but a clock that is not set right, and is never regulated, is never right at any time during the whole twenty-four hours.

The regulator keeps the clock going right, and is therefore of great importance in the clock's machinery.

And here we learn our third lesson from "looking at the clock."

We may go too fast towards sin, or too slowly towards our duty.

Therefore God has given to each of us a regulator. St. John said of our Lord Jesus Christ, "That was the true light which lighteth every man that cometh into the world."

That regulator of our lives and character which is implanted in every one of us is our conscience. It is the rule of right within us. It is or ought to be as much the regulator of our characters, as the mysterious regulator of a clock is the secret unseen power which directs and rules the clock's action.

This is the third lesson which we learn from "looking at the clock."

IV.

Fourthly, we learn that the regulator of a clock is of no use without a key to the clock.

It is not every key which will wind up every clock. Every clock must have its own special key which will fit it. Some keys are too large, other keys are too small. Sometimes it is a very hard thing to find a key which will fit our watch. The face of the clock may be perfect; the hands may be right; the regulator may be in perfect order, and yet the clock will not go unless it has a key to wind it up.

Now, how is it with us? What is the best key which fits into our hearts and winds them up so that they will keep good time?

Let me tell you. A great many years ago

the Moravians in Germany sent out some missionaries into Greenland to convert the poor Esquimau people out there. These missionaries began by preaching to them about the divine attributes of God, and the arguments which prove the being of God.

It was very good preaching, but somehow or other it did not take hold of the natives, and nobody was converted. After preaching in this way for about a year they thought they would try another kind of preaching.

So they began to tell these poor heathen Greenlanders about the love of the Lord Jesus Christ in coming down into this world to save it.

Instantly the Greenlanders became interested. This was something they could take hold of, and very soon a great number came to the missionaries to be baptized. *This key fitted into their hearts.* The other key did not fit at all. It could not make them go. This key fitted their needs exactly.

My dear children, the law of obedience to God through the love of Jesus Christ, is the one key which will fit into all our hearts. This is the key which will wind us up to the completest service of our Father in Heaven. Nothing on earth will make us go, and will help us to keep better time than love to Jesus Christ our Saviour.

V.

Fifthly, we learn that the key of a clock is of no use unless it is used.

If you keep the key hanging up on a nail and never apply it to your clock it will be of no use to you. You might just as well have a wooden key.

If you have a horse and never use him: if you have a book and never read it; if you have a new suit of clothes and never wear them, they will never do you any good; you might just as well be without them.

And, my dear children, if you don't make any use of the Lord Jesus Christ, you cannot expect that he will do you any good.

I have seen people in Europe in the great cathedrals kneeling down and praying to a wooden image of the Saviour on the cross.

Perhaps you may say, how foolish it is of them to pray to a wooden image. But is your Lord Jesus Christ a real Saviour to you, or is He only a wooden Jesus? Do you go to him in your troubles? Do you make use of Him? Do you ask Him to help you in your daily life, with your duties, with your studies, and with your many temptations?

How can you expect your clock to go unless you use your key?

How can you expect to be a true Christian unless you make use of the Lord Jesus Christ?

These then are the lessons which we learn from looking at the clock:

1st. The face of the clock is of no use without the hands of a clock.

2d. The hands of a clock are of no use without the works of a clock.

3d. The works of a clock are of no use without the regulator.

4th. The regulator of a clock is of no use without a key to the clock.

5th. The key of a clock is of no use unless it is used.

Or in other words, these are the lessons of our subject:

1. What we do with our hands shows itself in our face.

2. What we do with our hands is either good or bad.

3. We either have or have not a regulator in our conscience.

4. Our conscience is either rusty or is ruled by the will of God.

5. Our conscience is of no use unless it is used.

You know if you keep a key hanging up on a nail all the time it is of no use. To be of any use you must use it.

A clock is of no use unless it is wound up, set, and is going.

Here in this world—old lesson though it be—there are only two keys which fit your nature. God and Satan are each trying to wind you up for the service of good or for the service of evil.

Dear children,—*make use of the Lord Jesus Christ just as you would use a key.* Use Him to set you going right and to wind you up day by day for God's service.

XV.

DOGS.

"Beware of dogs."—PHILLIPPIANS iii. 2.

"BEWARE of the dog"—is an old piece of advice. In the ruins of Pompeii the traveller to-day comes across this Latin motto in front of one of the old Roman houses, "Cave Canem," or, beware of the dog.

We do not see this sign as often now-a-days as we used to do in days gone by. Either the dogs are not as fierce as they used to be, or else people are not so much afraid of them, or perhaps the day for using the dog as a scare-crow has passed by.

The Jews were not fond of horses or dogs. In the book of Deuteronomy we read these words, "Thou shalt not bring the price of a dog into the house of the Lord thy God for any vow." That is, the Jews were not allowed to give a dog tax for any missionary or charitable purpose.

The prophet Isaiah says in a certain place, in speaking of the false shepherds, "They are all dumb dogs, they cannot bark, sleeping, lying down, loving to slumber. Yea, they are greedy dogs which can never howl enough, and they are shepherds that cannot understand."

When St. Paul said, "Beware of dogs," he was writing to the Christians at Philippi. He meant by dogs, bad men, or men who gave trouble. He knew very well what it was to have a crowd of barking, biting men at his heels, who were like a pack of howling dogs after him. His foes pursued him and followed him from one place to another, like hounds after their prey. So he said to his followers at Philippi, "Beware of dogs," meaning thereby, beware of those men who will pursue you and hunt after you, as dogs never give up the chase, and follow with eager search the scent of the game.

Now, what kind of dogs ought we to beware of? Let us look at some of the specimens in this moral dog-show to-day.

I.

Beware of the snarling dogs.

There are some little dogs who do not bite much, and can never do any great harm, who yet keep up a snapping kind of bark all the time.

Everybody about them is kept in a state of discomfort. The cows go for them with their horns, but can never toss them. The horses paw at them, but can never kick them. The barnyard fowls run away from them as fast as they can get off the ground, and every one is made uncomfortable by the presence of these snarling dogs.

Beware of these snarling dogs.

Don't have snarling companions: don't get into the company of snapping dogs, or else you too will become one of the pack.

Don't encourage a "snarling habit." Don't argue with snarling dogs; let them alone. The more you talk with them, the more they will snarl at you. The only way to stop a snarling dog is to stoop down and pick up a stone and hit him, so that his snarl is turned into a yelp. The only way to stop a snarling boy or man is to hit his conscience with some moral duty. Then his snarling stops and he runs away to do his duty. Beware then, first of all, of "snarling dogs."

II.

Beware of mongrel dogs.

Some dogs are open-hearted and honest, and will look you full in the eye, like the honest dogs they really are. I have seen colly dogs and grayhounds which have had the most lovely, tender, beautiful eyes, all full of soul and sentiment and moral sense. Then there are other dogs which are sulking, cowardly, sneaking dogs. They will wait their time until they can get a chance to growl at you, or bite you, or run off with your dinner on the sly. These sneaking dogs are nearly always mongrels. That is, they have got no good blood in them; they haven't any pedigree. Nobody knows who their parents or relations are, or what their bringing up has been. These mongrel dogs run the street by day and night; eat what they can steal or pick up, sleep wherever they can find a box to sleep in, and finally are caught by the dog-catcher, are placed in the pound for one week, and are then poisoned.

There are mongrel men and mongrel boys. Mongrel people are those who have no plan or purpose in life; who live from hand to mouth, and who never can tell from one day to another where their money is to come from or how they are going to get their daily food. Those people live in the streets, and in their friends' and neighbors' houses. They seem to have no homes of their own. They beg or borrow money; but are averse to doing a day's hard work. They have no principles or guiding habits; they do not move in any direction, they drift with the tide of people; keep in the midst of the crowd, live a kind of circus life, and at last are caught in some great scrape or trouble and die a miserable or ignominious death.

Children, beware of these dogs; do not associate with these mongrels, lest you become one of this same class.

III.

Beware of mad-dogs.

There is nothing more dreadful in all the list of diseases than the awful disease of hydrophobia, which rises from the virus or poison, coming from the bite of a mad-dog.

We always give a mad-dog plenty of room in the road. If a tree is near, it is a wise thing to climb up the tree. If a fence or a wall is close at hand, the most prudent thing we can do is to jump over the wall or get behind the fence. The mad-dog with froth and foam at his lips, and with his tongue hanging out his jaws is an ugly customer to meet. If he should pierce our flesh with his poisoned teeth we are at once candidates for Pasteur's treatment, if he can save us even then.

Nothing is more terrible in the crowded

street on a hot and muddy dogday in August than to hear the cry of "Mad-dog! Mad-dog!"

Beware of mad men and fierce and passionate boys. There is murder hidden in anger. There is death concealed in the fury and passion of hate.

Cain was a murderer in spirit before he killed his brother Abel, by the side of his upraised altar. Jesus said that whosoever hated his brother without a cause was a murderer. St. John says in his first Epistle, "Whosoever hateth his brother is a murderer; and ye know that no murderer hath eternal life abiding in him."

It is said of Julius Cæsar, that when he was provoked he used to repeat the whole Roman alphabet before he suffered himself to speak.

I was reading not long ago about a Scotch gardener who had a very fiery temper. He married a milkmaid who used to storm at the cows and get very angry at them. Everybody said that when they got married they would have terrible times, and would lead a cat and dog life. But instead of this they lived very happily together. At last one of the neighbors said to the wife, "Jennie, how is it that you and your husband get on so well together? We all supposed that you would have a very stormy time with your husband."

"Ach, dear no," replied Jennie. "I get angry, and Sandy gets angry, but we've made it a rule *never both to be angry at the same time.*"

Here is another story about the way in which one of these mad-dogs got over his attacks of anger.

A deacon, naturally a high-tempered man, was accustomed to beat his oxen over the head, as all his neighbors did. When he became a Christian, his cattle became remarkably docile. A friend inquired into the secret. "Why," said the deacon, "formerly, when my oxen were a little contrary, I flew into a passion, and beat them unmercifully. This made the matter worse. Now when they do not behave well, I go behind the load, and sit down and sing Old Hundred. I don't know how it is, but the psalm tune has a surprising effect on my oxen."

Children, beware of these mad-dogs! try to tame your tempers and they won't hurt you.

IV.

Beware of stubborn dogs.

The bull-dog is the type of the stubborn dog. He hangs on to whatever he has taken in his grip, whether he is in the right or in the wrong. He is a big, stubborn, pugnacious dog. There is no arguing or coaxing with a bull-dog. When he gets his jaw fastened to an adversary, one or the other of them has got to die.

Persevering people are all right, but stubborn people are all wrong.

A mule might be a heroic animal if he were only persevering; but there is nothing heroic about a mule, because a mule is not persevering, he is only stubborn. A stubborn man is one who will not give in even when he knows that he is wrong. Stubborn people are very hard to get on with. They are very unpleasant to have as companions. Beware of these stubborn people. Beware of the stubborn dogs.

V.

Beware of fancy dogs.

There are some dogs which are good for nothing. They have to be washed and cared for and only live to be petted. They can't do anything for a living. They never could catch a mouse or a rat, or defend the house at night. If a burglar should get in the house at night they would be of no more use than a canary-bird. At the great dog show in New York last spring, I saw a great number of these fancy dogs, poodles and lapdogs and King Charles spaniels.

Now, there are a great many children, and a great many grown up people, who are just like these fancy dogs. There is no use for them. They have nothing to do:

they can't take care of themselves, and if they are not spoiled and petted they do not know what to do with themselves.

These people have no true idea of what the meaning of life is, or of what the world really is. They want everybody to come to their dog basket and pet them and coax them, and give them cake and candy, and if they do not get what they want they whine and are miserable.

This is a very poor kind of companion. Beware of these merely ornamental people.

Beware of fancy dogs.

VI.

Beware of dogs which are blood-hounds.

Blood-hounds are fearful animals. They have got the scent in them for human blood. They were used in old times in tracking runaway slaves in the South and in following up the wandering serfs or slaves in Russia. They pursue their victims to death. They never lose their scent. They never get off their trail.

They bark and bay through the forest and over the lake, and never give up until they have tracked their victim down to death.

And there are men and women to-day, my dear children, who will pursue you to bitter death. The drunkard, the gambler, the fast liver, the jockey, the sensualist, the destroyer of man's honor and woman's innocence—are blood-hounds. They are after their prey continually. They will not stop until they have killed their victim.

When I was in St. Louis over a year ago, I stayed at the same hotel where Maxwell the murderer had killed his victim and had packed his body in the trunk. I was at the Southern Hotel when the body of poor Preller was found in room 144. That companion of his, the guilty murderer, had planned how he was to get Preller's money, for weeks ahead. He had hunted his victim down, just as the blood-hounds used to do in the fearful days of slavery in the South.

Beware! beware! of these companions. Beware of the blood-hounds of the soul!

And now in closing let me say, "Beware of all dogs."

These are some of the dogs we ought to be afraid of.

1st. Snarling dogs.
2d. Mongrel dogs.
3d. Mad-dogs.
4th. Stubborn dogs.
5th. Fancy dogs.
6th. Blood-hounds.

David says in one of his psalms, "Dogs have compassed me round about."

These dog-like companions are around at every turn in life. Let us seek by the help of our Lord Jesus Christ to get the victory over all our temptations and our tempters. And thus it will not be in vain that we have heeded the advice of the apostle Paul, "Beware of Dogs."

XIII.

THE POWER OF A FACT.

"And they compel one Simon a Cyrenian—the father of Alexander and Rufus, to bear his cross."—St. Mark xv. 21.

THERE are a great many kinds of power in the world. There is the power which is in nature, in the gale at sea, in the tornado upon land, in the bolt of lightning in the thunderstorm.

Then there is the power which is in human machinery, in the electric plant, in the printing press, in the steam engine, and in the water wheel.

I want to speak to you to-day about another kind of power from either of these. I mean the power which there is in a fact.

This sermon then is about "THE POWER OF A FACT."

Let me tell you what I mean by this. All you school children know what it is to study American history.

You read in your history about the Boston tea party, and how the Americans, disguised as Indians, threw the tea overboard into Boston Harbor. Or you read about Washington crossing the Delaware to fight the Hessians at Trenton, or going to Cambridge to take command of the army there, or of Abraham Lincoln raising the flag on Independence Hall on Washington's birth-day, February 22d, 1861, as he was on his way to Washington to be inaugurated as President, at the breaking out of the civil war. Perhaps you may have seen pictures in your school-books of these different events; and these pictures may have helped you to remember the facts of history, for there is great power in pictures. But now, suppose you go to Trenton, and see for yourself the exact spot where Washington crossed on that stormy Christmas Eve, or you go out to Cambridge and see with your own eyes the great elm-tree under which

Washington assumed command of the Continental army, or you go down to the wharf where the tea was thrown overboard, and the old fact of history comes to you with a new meaning as you see for yourself the very spot where the event took place.

Then the power which there is in the fact of history comes home to you with a new meaning. You believe the far off fact because you have seen for yourself the place where the event took place.

I have read, in the latest American history, about Mr. Lincoln raising the flag on Independence Hall. But this fact of history is made more real to me because as a college boy I saw him, with my own eyes, pull the cord which raised the flag to the spire over the Liberty Bell on Independence Hall, on February 22d, 1861—just before the civil war began.

'In an old palace at Delft in Holland, visitors are shown the very spot where the assassin Balthazar Gérard stood when he shot down the faithful father of his people, William of Orange. At Holyrood palace in Edinburgh, travellers can see the back stairs where Rizzio, the secretary of Mary Queen of Scots, was stabbed, and down which his dead body was dragged.

And at Canterbury Cathedral in England, the very step in the chancel is shown to tourists on which the axe of the three assassins clave in two the skull of Thomas à Becket, as he was saying Vespers at the altar in the Cathedral.

There is a great power in the fact of *a fact*. Nothing can ever rob us of the fact that the event has certainly taken place.

And when we think of that greatest event of all this world's history, the presence of Jesus Christ among men, nothing can ever rob us of the power which there is in the fact that He was once in this world where we are, and walked this same earth on which our feet now tread.

Nothing can ever wipe away the fact, that once on a certain day in the world's history His blood-drops, from the cross on which He was hanging, fell upon a certain place called the place of a skull.

That is a fact, and there is power in that event considered simply in the light *that it is a fact*.

This sermon to-day is about "the power of a fact." "And they compel one Simon a Cyrenian,......the father of Alexander and Rufus, to bear his cross."

The story taken from St. Mark's Gospel is as follows.

When Jesus was led out to be crucified, he staggered and fell on the way under the heavy weight of his cross.

In the crowd which was looking on at the long procession wending its way to Calvary was a strong looking man from Africa, Simon by name, from the country in Egypt called Cyrene. When Jesus sank under his load, suffering as He was from the weakness of the long night spent in the Garden of Gethsemane and before Pilate and Herod and the High-priest, the soldiers laid hold upon this strong looking man, with his swarthy, dusky face, and compelled him to take up the cross of Jesus and carry it to Mt. Calvary. This Simon was called Niger, or "Black," because of his dark complexion. He is mentioned both by St. Matthew and St. Luke, and St. Mark gives the account of him which we find in this text. "And they compel one Simon a Cyrenian, who passed by, coming out of the country, the father of Alexander and Rufus, to bear his cross."

This Simon was well known, no doubt, after this event in Jerusalem, but his boys, Alexander and Rufus, in all probability went to Rome to live, for in St. Paul's Epistle to the Romans, we find him greeting one Rufus as "chosen in the Lord." Now, the Gospel by St. Mark was written for the Gentile Christians; and especially to those who lived at Rome. The people in Rome would not know who this Simon the Cyrenian was, but they would know who Alexander and Rufus were, for they in all probability lived there. So when St. Mark spoke of this Simon the Cyrenian who bore the cross of Jesus, he added, for the sake of those persons who lived in Rome and knew Simon's sons: "he was the father of Alexander and Rufus."

'Go back with me then, my dear children, to this far-off scene which St. Mark here describes. There is in Antwerp a picture by Rubens of this scene of Simon carrying the cross of Jesus.

"It represents," says a certain writer describing it, "our Lord bearing His cross on the way to Calvary, when Simon of Cyrene is met coming out of the country with his two boys, Alexander and Rufus, and he is compelled for a while to bear the cross and ease the shoulder of Jesus, galled by its great weight. After a while the cross is once more given to Christ to carry, and we see the two boys looking with awe-struck eyes at the pale face of Jesus, with the blood trickling down from the thorn-crowned temples. There is pity trembling in the eyes and on the lips of the lads, mingled with curiosity, and little Rufus, unable to bear the sight, is bursting into tears and is hiding his face on his brother's breast."

This then is the picture, and this is the story, which has given us our sermon today.

Those boys, Alexander and Rufus, never could forget that scene when Jesus fell under his cross, and their father was seized, standing as he was by the wayside, and was made to carry the Saviour's cross.

Perhaps there were many children that day looking on at the long procession through the streets of Jerusalem, wending its way to that green hill outside the city wall. Some of them no doubt grew up and forgot all about Jesus. Some may have thought of Him only as one out of many prisoners whom they had seen led to execution. But Alexander and Rufus never forgot that day. They never forgot that for a little while their father took the place of Jesus, on that journey to Calvary.

They became followers of Jesus, and many years after this event they were known as

Christians at Rome; and to one of them, Rnfus, the great apostle St. Paul sent a loving message, saying that he was "chosen in the Lord."

This scene and this story then give us our subject to-day. Let us now see what lessons we learn from this subject of, "*The Power of a Fact.*"

I.

First. *The facts of our childhood are the facts which have come to stay.*

The memory is the most wonderful thing in all our nature. It is like the double entry books which the clerks keep in their desks and offices. Everything which we do, every transaction of our life, gets recorded in the books of our memory. And what is called the opening of the books at the day of Judgment may be, after all, but the opening of the long-forgotten books of memory, just as a bookkeeper goes to his great ledger-book, and opens it to find some recorded sale which he knows he will discover in the book, though he cannot remember the event himself.

And it is the facts of our childhood which are written deepest upon the memory. We are young and fresh and tender in our childhood hours, and the things which happen to us then make the deepest impression upon our memory. When a cake or a loaf of bread is put into the oven to bake, you know it is soft and tender. You can write your name on the dough or can make pictures of animals or men upon it. But when it comes out of the oven it is hard and baked and dry.

It will not take any new impressions then. *The heat has made a crust* come over the tender dough.

Well! in very much this same way, life is like an oven to us. The heat of life brings out a hard crust over us. It is a very difficult thing to make any impression on our nature after we have got our manhood's crust on us.

I was reading the other day about a burglar out in St. Louis. He was a young man who had joined a gang of thieves. One night as he was boring with his augur from an old wareroom into a store-room where a great many valuables were kept, he heard a mother in the room next to him singing to her baby in the cradle, Dr. Watts' nursery hymn:

> "Hush, my dear, lie still and slumber,
> Holy angels guard thy bed,
> Heavenly blessings without number
> Gently fall upon thy head."

The partition wall was very thin. He heard this mother singing the very hymn and tune which he remembered his mother had sung when he was a little fellow in her arms. *The books were opened.* The record book of memory was the record book of judgment. He excused himself from the rest of his companions and ran down the rickety stairs of the old ware-room until he reached the front door, when he threw down his valise with his "jimmy" and other burglar's tools and ran off—never to be a robber any more.

That hymn had power in it; it was the power which there is in a fact. That fact of his early childhood was a fact which he had thought was forgotten, but it was after all a fact that had come to stay.

In the same way, the fact which Alexander and Rufus saw, when their father, Simon, carried the cross of Jesus, was a fact which remained with them throughout their whole lives. They never could forget it. It was one of the facts of their childhood which had come to remain with them through life.

And we all have such facts about us continually. There is power in the facts of our life. There is the greatest of all power in the facts of our life as children, for these facts are the facts which have come to stay with us.

II.

The facts of our childhood are the seeds of our after life.

A seed is a wonderful thing. It is the

model of the plant or tree or flower which comes up out of it from the ground. Whenever we paint or draw or work or write we want a model. There was a poor weaver who came to me a year ago, to tell me that he had invented a new loom with a new kind of "shut off" motion. He felt sure that if he could only get a patent on it he would be able to make a great deal of money.

So Mathew the weaver and I talked it all over, and drew up papers and plans, and sent to Washington to the Patent office there for a "Patent." But we found that before we could get a "Patent," we would have to send on a model to go into the office there.

At last Mathew the weaver came one night to the house with his model. It was in wood, and was covered over with gold dust so as to look very beautiful. This model was an exact miniature of the patent loom. It was the germ seed of which the loom was the flower.

Now, my dear children, what we are in childhood, we are in after life.

The poet Wordsworth says, "The child is the father of the man."

You know we always think that a man is the father of his child. But in reality the child is the father of the man, for what we are in our childhood we shall be when we grow up to be men and women. And so it happens that the facts of our childhood are the seeds of our after life. If you open a seed, such as a kernel of corn, or a grain of wheat, or an acorn, you will find in the heart of the seed the model of the plant. A tiny ear of corn will be seen in the grain of corn, a tiny ear of wheat will be seen in the piece of wheat, a tiny oak tree will be seen in the very heart of the acorn. These seeds are the beginnings of all things to the plants. They are the bottom facts of their existence. And the facts of our childhood are the seeds of our after life. What kind of facts are happening to you, my dear children? The things which are happening to you now are the seeds which are being sown for the days which are to come afterwards!

III.

Good deeds done, are never thrown away.

That was a good deed which Simon the Cyrenian did for the suffering Saviour. We do not know with what motive he carried the cross of Christ. Perhaps he may have felt for Him in His sufferings. Perhaps he may have shown his sympathy for Jesus by some kind look in his eye. However this may be, he stooped down and took the heavy beam of wood upon his own shoulders and Jesus was relieved of His burden.

Alexander and Rufus saw all this. They saw their father do this act of kindness for the thorn-crowned prophet. They saw him stoop under the weight of the cross. Perhaps they heard him pant for breath. They heard the noise which the end of the cross made as it scraped the ground along which it was dragged. They saw the long line which the heavy beam made along the turf and sand until they came to Calvary. They saw their father at the hill of Crucifixion exchange places with Jesus again. Perhaps they held on to their father's hands, glad to have him once more with them, while the soldiers nailed Jesus to the cross. All this they never, never forgot.

We do not know what kind of a Christian Alexander was. St. Paul says of Rufus that "he was chosen in the Lord."

I rather think they must both have been good men, or St. Paul would not have sent a message to them, or have remembered them in his letter to the Christians at Rome.

At any rate, this we know, the good deeds which we do for others, the kind actions, the loving words, the gentle tones, the unselfish things which we do for those about us, never can be forgotten. We think that they are dead and forgotten. But they live over and over again in the lives and memories of those whom we have helped.

I have no doubt that Alexander and Rufus, if they were good and kind to the poor saints who were in Rome, were good and kind, first of all, because they remembered how, when they were boys looking on at the procession to Mount Calvary, they had seen their father, Simon the Cyrenian, carrying the cross of their Lord Jesus Christ.

These then are the lessons which this subject teaches us.

I.

The facts of our childhood are the facts which have come to stay.

II.

The facts of our childhood are the seeds of our after life.

III.

Good deeds done are never thrown away.

Alexander and Rufus, looking on at their father carrying the cross of Jesus, never forgot that scene. It lived over and over again in their after lives. The power which it exerted in their days of manhood was, the power which there always is in a *Fact.*

XVII.

SATAN'S FISHING TACKLE.

"They take up all of them with the angle, they catch them in their net, and gather them in their drag."—HABAKKUK i. 15.

THE Jewish people had very little to do with two things of which the American people are very fond,—fast horses and fast ships. Going down into the sea in ships, or going down into Egypt with horses, always seemed to the Jews to be the height of uncertainty and risk, and thus it came to pass that ships and horses always stood as the highest symbols possible of folly.

But the prophet Habakkuk, who lived about six hundred years before Christ, had perhaps seen some of his fellow-countrymen fishing for deep sea fish in the Mediterranean, or on the lake of Galilee, in the North Country, and had made a note of the three ways of catching fish. He saw the fishermen about him catching fish in these three ways: first, by angling for them; secondly, by catching them in a net; and thirdly, by driving them together by means of a drag.

And then, when he looked about him, and saw his fellow-countrymen rushing into sin, and being caught by temptation and dragged into evil, he said they were as "the fishes of the sea, as the creeping things that have no ruler over them. They take up all of them with the angle, they catch them in their net, they gather them in their drag."

Fishing and fishing tackle form a great department of life. There is a great deal of water on this globe of ours, and where there is a great deal of water there will be a great many fish, and where there are a great many fish there will be a great many fishermen.

But after all there are only three ways of catching fish: by angling for them, by getting them into the net, and by dragging for them. Sometimes the Indians spear fish as they go over the waterfalls. This is the way the Penobscot Indians used to fish along the rivers in Maine, but this was only for a certain kind of fish, the salmon, and was only practised by a few Indian tribes.

Our subject to-day is, "Satan's Fishing Tackle." One of the old Church Fathers said that "Satan is the ape of God." He meant by this that Satan imitated whatever God did. You know how many counterfeit things there are in the world. On all sorts of packages to-day, such as soap, perfumery, cologne, and medicines, you will find the words, "Beware of imitations," "None genuine without our signature."

God strives to do a certain thing, and then this evil principle in the world which we call Satan imitates this act.

God strives to win men, and Satan strives to do the same. God strives to save men, and Satan strives to destroy them. God uses all sorts of means to catch men; Satan uses all sorts of instruments to do the same.

This world in which we live is good or

bad, according as we use it. We can put a hook in the things about us and can catch them for God's service, or we can put a hook in them and catch them for the service of sin.

Art, music, pleasure, books, society, fame, glory, power, wealth, pictures, and everything which makes this world lovely is only bad when Satan puts his hook through them as bait, and lands us in his own boat with his own fishing tackle.

The one way to catch fish is to have plenty of bait. There are a great many things in this world which are good enough in themselves, only, if we look sharp we shall surely see Satan's hook under them. These attractions and pleasures of life are the things which he uses for bait. You children who fish and are fond of fishing, know just how this is. Some fish will bite at one kind of bait and some at another. There are times when trout fish will bite at worms. There are other times when they will bite only at flies.

Crabs bite at a piece of red flannel It is the red color which attracts their eye. Bluefish bite at a metal squid. It is the shining, bright, silvery steel gliding through the water which makes them snap at it. "They take up all of them with the angle."

And men and women are very much like the fishes of the sea. They get caught by the baits of Satan in very much the same way that fish are caught by the hook concealed beneath the bait. All the temptations which we find around us in our every-day life are Satan's baits. We see the bait and not the hook. But if we yield to sin, the bait is gone in a moment, and the cruel hook is felt.

There are three ways in which we are caught by Satan's fishing tackle:

I.

First of all, there is the way in which we are caught by the angle. Some fish, such as salmon and trout, bite at the bait. They rise out of the water to snap at the hook concealed beneath the fly or the worm. Other fish, like the heavy flounder, merely suck in the hook lazily, and happen, as it were, to get caught.

And there are certain people in the world who seem to bite at sin for the love which they have for sin. It is one thing to sin because we are tempted, or because we are in the company of others who are sinning. It is quite another thing to sin because we want to sin,—to bite at the bare hook of sin itself.

I was talking the other day with a very good person, when all of a sudden this very good person said, "I don't know why I should feel as I do, but I do want to do something wicked,"—"Do something wicked?" I asked. "Why do you want to do something wicked?"—"I don't know," replied this very good person, "unless it is Satan trying to make me bite at his bare hook."

Well, my dear children, Satan does make us at times not only do wrong, but *want to do wrong*. That is the hard part of it.

And that is why we must have the grace of our Lord Jesus Christ to keep us from the evil forces around us. The Apostle calls this evil tendency within us "Satan's devices." He has his arts, and snares, and tricks. He takes us up with his temptations, and we take up with his angle."

"When I see the fisher bait his hook," says an old writer, "I think of Satan's subtle malice, who sugars over his poisoned hooks with seeming pleasure. Thus Eve's apple was candied with divine knowledge. 'Ye shall be as gods, knowing good and evil.' When I see the fish fast hanged, I think upon the covetous worldling who leaps at the profit without considering the danger. Thus Achan takes the gold and the garment, and never considers that his life must answer for it. If Satan be such a fisher of men, it is good to look before we leap."

The first way in which we are caught by Satan's fishing tackle is the way in which we bite at sin, the way in which "we take up with the angle."

II.

Secondly, there is the way in which we are caught by the net.

When a fish is caught in a net, he is caught because he is in company. A fish will bite at a hook alone, but a fish will never go into a net alone. Fish go in shoals or schools, birds go in a flock, cattle go in a herd. When animals go together they always head the same way. Birds don't fly north, south, east and west. They always fly in the same direction. Cows in a pasture field do not graze in opposite ways. They always head together—up a field or down a field.

And we, my dear children, act in very much the same way as the beasts of the field, the birds of the air, and the fish of the sea. When we go wrong and get astray, we go wrong because we are in wrong company. The poor fish when they are caught in the net are all caught together. They flap and flounder around, but it is all in vain. The net gathers tightly about them, and soon they are breathing out their dying gasps in the bottom of the fisherman's boat. "They gather them in their net."

It is a good thing for us every little while to see how we are heading and who our companions are, for we very often are tempted to wrong-doing simply by the wrong-doing of our friends and companions.

Boys and girls! look well to your companions. See to it that they are not leading you into some net.

III.

Thirdly, there is the way in which we are caught by the drag.

A drag is a sort of a net with hooks and weights, which is drawn along the bottom of a lake or river, and which gathers the fish into it before they know it. The drag sweeps the bed of the stream, and collects everything which it can find, good or bad. If a fish who was caught by a drag could talk, and we were to say to him, "Will you be good enough, Mr. Fish, to tell us how you came to be caught in that way?" he would say, in reply, "My dear friends, I *was dragged into it*." "They gather them in their drag."

And in this same way we get dragged into sin before we know it. We are taken by surprise very often, and feel ourselves weak in the presence of some tempter, or some one with a commanding will, who is influencing us, and we get into sin and wrong-doing before we know it. Some stronger nature than ours influences us, and we in our weakness give way. Look at Simon Peter in Pilate's judgment hall. He really did not mean to deny his Lord. He did not plan out his denial, as Judas did. He was taken by surprise. He was dragged into his sin before he knew it. He was caught, not by Satan's hook or by Satan's net; he was caught by Satan's drag. The servant girl laughed at him, and her companions jeered at him for being a friend of Jesus, and Simon Peter yielded to his surroundings, and was dragged by them into his denial of his Master.

SATAN'S FISHING TACKLE. 253

Look out for the drag, children! Look out for this way of being carried off your feet into sin before you know it.

Don't take up with the angle. Don't take up with the net. Don't take up with the drag.

These, then, are the lessons of our sermon to-day about Satan's fishing tackle:

First. There is the way in which we are caught by the *angle*, or the way we have of *biting* at sin.

Secondly. There is the way in which we are caught by the *net*, or the way we have of going in the *company* of other sinners.

Thirdly. There is the way in which we are caught by the *drag*, or the way we have of being *dragged* into sin.

I was reading the other day about a true answer which one sinner made to another. A drunken student, trying to excuse his intoxication, said, "I don't know how it is that I am here in this condition, but now that I am in for it, I mean to go the whole figure.

One might as well be killed for a sheep as for a lamb. I had no idea of getting into such a spree. I cannot tell what brought it about. *I suppose Satan tempted me."*—"Poh!" said another, "he didn't do any such thing. Do you want to know how it happened with me? I went up to my room and read awhile, and then grew restless and wanted some exciting pleasures, and, *after waiting for Satan to come to me, I came out in search of him, and here I am.*" The devil is easily found by those who seek him, and it is a mean, cowardly piece of business to lay the blame where it does not belong, and say that he tempts us when we run to put ourselves in the way of temptation.

Children, be careful how you get into that current of life in which you know that Satan is fishing, for he has all sorts of fishing tackle, and will get you by hook or by crook if he can.

Beware of Satan's *hook*, covered by the tempting bait; beware of Satan's *net*, which those who enter do not see; beware of Satan's drag, which will sooner or later, haul in all who are enclosed by it.

The angle; the net; and the drag; these are around us at every turn in life.

Dear children, don't let go the help which comes to you from our Lord Jesus Christ, for without that help we are in continual danger of falling into the hand of Satan— the Evil Fisherman.

XVIII.

THE MAN WHO SAVED AND THE MAN WHO TAXED.

"It came to pass in those days, that there went out a decree from Cæsar Augustus that all the world should be taxed."—ST. LUKE ii. 1.

IN the beautiful gallery of the Pittsfield Athenæum, there is the bust of Cæsar Augustus, the Roman Emperor, when he was a boy, and the statue of the same Emperor when he was a man. I have often watched these two faces, in their white stucco material, and have noticed how the uncertain lines in the face of the boy have become hardened out in the face of the man. The beautiful face of the boy Augustus, that happy, favored nephew of the great Julius Cæsar, becomes in the man the hard, cruel and selfish face of the Roman Emperor. The history of the Emperor Augustus is as follows:

When his great uncle, Julius Cæsar, was at the height of his power, he adopted this youth, whose name was Octavius or Octavianus, and made him his heir. When Julius Cæsar was assassinated in the Senate, a triumvirate of Roman Generals was formed, consisting of Lepidus, Antony and Octavius. After various fortunes, in which Antony linked his career with that of Cleopatra, Queen of Egypt, a great battle was fought at Actium, in the year B. C. 31, which left Octavius, who was always a child of fortune, sole ruler of Rome, and consequently of the world. Then the Roman Senate voted that he should become Emperor of Rome, and that divine honors should be paid to him. Thereupon he took the name of "Augustus"—from the auguries or august honors which were paid to him—and in this way what was called the golden or Augustan Age began.

The "Augustan Age' in France was when Louis XIV. was king, and the period of

The Man who Taxed.

Queen Anne was called the "Augustan Age" in England.

The Emperor Augustus was a friend to learning, and a great patron of the arts. The celebrated poets Virgil, Horace and Ovid, and the historian, Livy, flourished during this "Augustan Age."

The Latin poet, Horace, wrote many odes at this period about the Great Augustus and his friend Macenas. When you boys come to study Latin for college you will have to translate these odes of the poet Horace.

In the 12th ode of the first book of Horace we find the Emperor Augustus described in these words:

"O thou son of Saturn, author and preserver of the human race, the protection of Cæsar is committed to thy charge by Fates: Thou shall reign supreme, with Cæsar for thy second; he shall rule the wide world with equty in subordination to thee."

Indeed many of the odes of this period, from the poets Virgil and Horace, speak of the great Augustus in the way in which King

David and his son Solomon are described in the Psalms, and in the way in which the Messiah of the Jews is mentioned by the prophet Isaiah.

Some of these odes sound very much like the words of that hymn which we sing at Christmas time:—

> "Hail to the Lord's anointed,
> Great David's greater Son:
> Hail in the time appointed,
> His reign on earth begun!
> He comes to break oppression,
> To set the captive free—
> To take away transgression,
> And rule in equity."

When Augustus was sixty-six years old, or ten years before his death, in the year 4, B. C. (four years before the date commonly called the Christian Era), he issued a decree that all the world should be taxed.

In the same year, in a stable belonging to an inn at the little town of Bethlehem, Jesus Christ was born!

We all know the story of His birth. We

always read it with joy and pleasure in the Services of Christmas time. Little did the great Augustus, in his palace at Rome, know of that event which took place in the far-off country of Judea, when he issued his decree—that all the world should be taxed. Herod, the King, at his court in Jerusalem; nobles in their chariots riding through the crowded streets of the city; soldiers hustling their way through the castle; priests and doctors around the steps of the temple, all were occupied with their different occupations, and little thought of the great event which happened in Bethlehem when Joseph and Mary were enrolled in their native town, and the child Jesus was born in the stable.

I want to speak to you to-day about the two great laws of our life, or what we learn from the man who *taxed*, and what we learn from the man who *saved*.

I

The first law of life is *the law of life for self*. Cæsar Augustus taxed people. He had them all enrolled in the towns where they belonged, and then everybody in the great Empire of Rome, which was all the world, was taxed. These taxes brought in a vast amount of money and material wealth, which went, as it was supposed, to support the government, but inasmuch as all the Cæsars grew very wealthy in office, these taxes in reality went into the coffers of those in power.

And this same decree very frequently goes forth from certain people to-day, that all their friends shall be taxed. All people who habitually think more of themselves than they do of others, *tax* their friends. If we think of our friends only in the way of what we can get out of them, that is not friendship, it is only the tax of Cæsar Augustus upon all the world. It is tyranny—not friendship.

Two children were playing not long ago, in a family sitting-room, when one of them said suddenly: "Jack, I wonder why Uncle Tom doesn't come to see us any more? He used to come a great deal, and I always loved to have him come; he used to tell us such funny stories. Do you know why he doesn't come here any more?"

"Yes," replied Jack; "I know the reason, it's because he's poor now."

"Poor?" asked Jack's brother Don, "poor? Why, what has that got to do with his coming here?"

"I don't know," replied Jack; "but I heard Aunt Maria say the other day that there was no use in asking Uncle Tom to come here any more, for they are very poor now and there was *nothing to be gotten out of them any more.*"

"There went forth a decree that all the world should be *taxed.*" Yes, there is a great deal of this domestic home-made taxing going on in our homes to-day. Boys and girls tax their visitors and their relatives and their friends. They tax their parents and get into the way of thinking that everybody exists on purpose to furnish a revenue for them. Cakes, candies, presents, spending money, all these are the taxes which boys and girls put upon their friends, when, like Cæsar Augustus, they obey the law of life for self and send forth a decree that all the world shall be taxed.

Now, my dear children, that is what I mean by the Cæsar Augustus kind of life. All the world is looked upon as a source of revenue or income for one's own self, and the law of life for self only, keeps sending forth this decree continually that all the world shall be taxed.

II.

The other law of life is the law of life for others.

When Jesus was born in Bethlehem there went forth a message of love that all the world should be saved. The angels sang in the heavens—"Glory to God in the highest, and on earth peace, good will toward men." The one law of the life of Jesus was the law of life for others. He bore the Cross not for himself, but for us. His whole life was spent in saving others, and helping others, and doing good to all who were around Him. He prayed upon the Cross for His murderers —"Father, forgive them," he said, "for they know not what they do!"

People to-day have forgotten all about Cæsar Augustus—the man who taxed the world for himself. But to-day the Lord Jesus Christ is loved and honored and served by millions of people who have been drawn to Him by the law of His life, that conquering law of all life, the law of life for others. Jesus said, "I, if I be lifted up, will draw all men unto me." And He has drawn the world to Him, and saved the world by the way in which He has lived and died in order to *bless* the world instead of living only to *tax* the world. And if we are the followers of the Lord Jesus Christ, we ought to have His spirit. St. Paul says in one place, "If any man have not the spirit of Christ, he is none of his." We want that spirit which saves and pleases; not that spirit which taxes and gives pain.

One of the legends of Scottish history tells

us, that while the great Earl of Douglas was living, he was the terror of all his enemies, and that his name carried fear and consternation wherever it went. Sir Walter Scott says that mothers used to sing to their children this lullaby:

> "Hush ye—hush ye—
> Little pet ye—
> Lie you still
> And don't you fret ye—
> The Black Douglas—
> Shall not get ye."

On his crest were written the words: "Thou shalt want ere I want." After his death his heart was taken out and preserved in a strong urn, and his followers used to carry it with them to battle. When they failed to carry the day, or when the battle was going against them, the man who carried the precious urn would hurl it into the enemy's ranks, crying out, "Remember the Black Douglas, his heart has gone before you."

Well! my dear children, in very much

this same way, if we want to keep very close to the life of our Lord Jesus Christ, we must follow His heart of love wherever we can find that heart loving and blessing the world. Let us save others instead of taxing them. Remember what power there is in a cheering word; in an act of kindness and love, in making the world better and brighter for our being in it, instead of making the world sad and sorrowful by the way we add to the taxes of life. Remember that the one only way to be loved is to love: the one only way to be blessed, is to bless, and remember this also, that whether we know it or not, and whether we realize it or not, it is a truth that whatsoever we sow that shall we reap. If we sow taxes, we shall reap taxes: if we sow blessings, we shall reap blessings.

These then are the two lessons of this subject. There are, after all, only two laws or principles by which we act in life. The first is the law of life for self. The second is the law of life for others.

Cæsar Augustus, the Roman Emperor,

thought only of himself. So he sent forth a decree that all the world should be taxed.

The Lord Jesus Christ, the son of a Galilean carpenter, thought only of others, so he sent forth a decree that all the world might be saved. Who cares for Cæsar Augustus now?

He is forgotten, while the little babe of Bethlehem, who was enrolled in Judea at the time of the taxing by Augustus, lives on in the hearts and lives of countless Christian followers.

Depend upon it, my dear children, it is better to do good than merely to get good. It is better to think of the good of others rather than the good of one's self. It is better to *save* people than it is to *tax* people.

XIX.

SCHOOL-BOY SAINTS.

"All the Saints salute you."—2 CORINTHIANS xiii. 13.

THIS sermon is about "School-boy Saints." I will tell you what I mean by this.

When an army is drawn up on dress parade to salute its commanding officer, the general, or commander, stands upon some prominent place, and the entire army files past it and salutes the commander as he stands with his staff around him. All the soldiers salute their officers by "presenting arms," or touching their caps, and in this way, as an army division passes its staff officers, all the troops salute them.

In very much this same way St. Paul says to the Corinthian Christians, "All the Saints salute you," that is all the Saints which are at Philippi salute you. St. Paul wrote this epistle from the city of Philippi, and in writing he sent his love and the love of all his fellow Philippian Christians, to the Christians of Corinth. It is as if all the different members of the Christian Church had passed by in a long review before the Church which was at Corinth, and had saluted it. Gray-haired old men and women; fathers and mothers, with their boys and girls, and with little infants in their arms, all passed by in a long procession, and saluted their brethren of the Church at Corinth. Somewhere in this long line there must have been children, for there were doubtless those who were baptized, when young, into the Christian Church. So then if there were young people there were undoubtedly boys and girls who were trying to be Christians, and these young Saints of Philippi saluted those of Corinth, when St. Paul wrote these words:

"All the Saints salute you."

Now, when I say "School-boy Saints," I mean, of course, boys and girls, all young people who are trying to be followers of the Lord Jesus Christ.

Let me tell you the story of the patron Saint of all school boys, and then find out the lessons which this subject teaches us. St. Nicholas, whom we always remember as the St. Nicholas or Santa Claus of Christmas time, was born in Patara, in Asia Minor, on the 6th of December, A. D. 343. He is known in Church history as the patron Saint of all school-boys. At last, in some way, when the story of St. Nicholas came into Germany, it became changed into the story or legend of Santa Claus, the jolly old Dutch Saint, who used to come down the chimney with all sorts of good gifts for the children. St. Nicholas was made Bishop of Myra when he was a boy, and after his life the practice became established, every now and then, of choosing boy Bishops.

When Nicholas was a young man at Patara, he became very fond of having boys come to his house to study with him. He seems to have had a great influence over boys, and to have been very popular with them. It was in this way that he became in after years the patron Saint of schoolboys.

Well; there is an old story that upon one occasion a very rich merchant sent his sons to be educated by St. Nicholas, at Patara. The boys stopped over night at an inn in the place. The keeper of this inn and his wife, finding that they were alone, and that they had money with them, planned to murder them at night. So at midnight, just before the time of cock-crowing, this wicked man and his wife entered their room and cut their throats with a carving knife.

For a long time it was supposed that the boys had been murdered by robbers in the night, but St. Nicholas boldly accused the inn-keeper and his wife, and the story is that they confessed their wickedness and suffered death. Another story is that St. Nicholas found the dead bodies of the two boys thrown into a ditch, with their necks all "scraggened," whatever that may mean, and that he touched their bleeding throats with holy oil, and prayed over them, and thus brought them back again to life. But of course this is all legend, and it is in this way that history becomes mixed with fable and loses its true character.

We find, however, that the custom of electing boys as Bishops, after the manner of St. Nicholas, extended until the year, A. D. 1550, when as King Edward I., the Plantaganet, was on his way to Scotland to fight the Scotch, he permitted one of the boy Bishops to say vespers before him in Durham Cathedral. At Salisbury Cathedral these boy Bishops had the power of making appointments and giving gifts, if any vacancies occurred during their reign.

But this custom of electing boy Bishops was stopped by the following Royal proclamation, which was published on July 22, 1542:

"And, whereas, heretofore, dyvers and many strange superstitions have been used in many parts of this Realme, as upon St. Nicholas, Holy Innocents, and the like, children be strangely decked and apparralled to counterfeit Priests and Bishops, the King's Majesty willeth that henceforth all such superstitions be left and clearly extinguished throughout the Realme and Dominion."

On December 5, 1554, there went forth another royal decree, that St. Nicholas, the patron Saint of boys, should not *go about*."

This refers to the beginning of that custom which became changed in Germany into the legend of Santa Claus coming on Christmas Eve with good gifts to children.

The old legend of St. Nicholas, which has become changed in our time into the fable of Santa Claus, is that St. Nicholas used to throw in their windows purses to poor girls the night before they were married, to be their marriage portions.

You all remember the Christmas song—

> "'Twas the night before Christmas, when all through the house
> Not a creature was stirring—not even a mouse,
> The stockings were hung by the chimney with care,
> In hopes that *St. Nicholas* soon would be there."

Well, this St. Nicholas of Christmas story is our old friend St. Nicholas of Asia, the patron Saint of school-boys.

The custom of filling children's stockings began in Italy and France, in the Middle Ages, in the convents; the poor nuns there believed that the good things which they received on Christmas Eve were the gifts of St. Nicholas.

An old legend of this period, in condemning this custom, uses the following words:—

> "St. Nicholas money used to give to maidens secretly,
> Who that he still may use his wonted liberality,
> The mothers all their children on this eve do cause to fast,
> And when they every one at night in senseless sleep do cast,

> Both apples, nuttes and peares they bring and other
>   things beside,
> As caps and shoes, and little coats, which secretly
>   they hide,
> And in the morning found they say that this St.
>   Nicholas brought,
> Thus tender minds to worship Saints and wicked
>   things are taught."

So much then for the boy Bishop—St. Nicholas—the patron Saint of school-boys.

Now what lesson do we learn from this old legend of the " School-boy's Saint ? "

I.

First. We learn that Saints can be made even out of school-boys. I say even out of *school-boys*. Think for a moment what an average school-boy is. He hates to go to school, and thinks it is very hard that he must go. He dislikes his teachers, and thinks that it is their one end and aim in life to give him long lessons. Acorns, nails, string, sling-shots, spools, stones, cast-off bits of iron, slate-pencils, and chewing-gum are in his pockets. He goes along dreamily to school, with thoughts of buccaneers and pirates in his brain, and with a strap full of books over his shoulder. He is the last kind of being one would ever think of converting into a Saint; yet all things are possible with God, and Saints have been known to be made even out of such school-boys.

"How do you know Tom is a Christian?" asked his brother Will of another boy they had been playing with.

"Oh, because," replied Will.

"Because," said his brother. "That's no reason. Give me a regular lawyer's reason."

"Well!" said Jack, Will's brother, "I stubbed his toes to-day in school, and I poured cold water down his back, and I walked him Spanish, and he never used a swear word once. Yes! I tell you Tom's a regular Saint—no mistake."

And it is of such changed lives as these St. Paul says: "All the Saints salute you."

II.

Secondly. We learn from this subject that school-boy Saints are splendid fellows.

School-boys have generally got very little money in their pockets, but they have a great deal of fine feeling in their hearts.

It is surprising how rapidly the money of boys disappears. A silver dollar gets very quickly broken into two halves; the two halves in the twinkling of an eye become two quarters, and the two quarters, before we know it, get very soon changed into nickels and dimes.

A boy cannot keep his money. He wants all sorts of things—in fact a long row of them, and he does not know which he wants most. He wants a Flobert rifle, and a velocipide, a sling, a dog, pigeons, rabbits, skates, a tool chest, tops, kites, and all sorts of things. He is always wanting some of these implements, and the consequence is he is always poor, and the missionary box suffers on Sunday morning on account of his weakened state of finances.

But after all it is a great deal better to have the dollar heart and the dime purse than it is to have the dime heart and the dollar purse. This was the way the man felt who told this story of himself.

"Once upon a time," he said, "I had a dollar in my heart and a dime in my purse. Then I wanted to have a dollar in my purse all the time. So after a while I grew rich and had a dollar in my purse every hour in the day, but at the same time I grew mean in my soul. In other words the dollar and the dime changed places. *The dime went into my heart at the very time that the dollar went into my purse.*"

Now, my dear children, it's a great thing in life to have and to keep this generous dollar kind of heart. If our heart is all right, everything is all right with us. King Solomon says, "Keep thy heart with all diligence, for out of it are the issues of life."

And when school-boys have got their hearts set right, and are trying to be strong and manly Christians, I tell you they are splendid fellows, and are just the kind St. Paul had in his mind when he said:

" All the Saints salute you."

III.

Lastly we learn that we can all be schoolboy kind of Saints if we try.

The difference between a Saint and a sinner is this, the Saint tries to give all he can, and a sinner tries to get all he can. If we keep thinking all the time of everything which we do in life and what we can get from it, we will soon become dwarfed and one-sided characters. But if we keep thinking, " What can I give to other people," we will find that we will grow in character in exact proportion to the way in which we do for others.

There was once a converted German who used to go about getting collections for his mission. He used to divide all the people he met into the two classes, of the " godly " people and the " ungodly ones."

"Has Mr. Jones given you anything?" a friend once asked.

"No," replied the German, "Mr. Jones is not a godly man, he gave me nothing."

"Has Mr. Brown given you anything?" asked his friend again.

"O yes," he replied, "Mr. Brown is a very godly man, he gave me ten dollars."

My dear children, let us all try to be school-boy Saints—Saints with dollar hearts and dollar pockets. Don't let the fact that we are trying to be Saints ever make us mean, or cramped, or narrow-hearted. God wants all His Saints to be large-minded, generous-hearted, and full of courage, zeal, and faith.

Remember then these three lessons which we learn from the story of St. Nicholas, the patron Saint of school-boys.

First.—God can make Saints even out of school-boys.

Second.—School-boy Saints are splendid fellows.

Third.—We can all be School-boy Saints if we try.

Let us try to follow the blessed Saints in all virtuous and godly living. Let us try to do good to others, and throw bright and cheery things into their life, as St. Nicholas did, and has been remembered as the kind-hearted friend of little children because of his kind deeds in this way.

Let us salute all God's Saints! Let us take off our hats to them. Let us present arms to them for all that they have done in the world, and in this way we 'will find ourselves among the ranks of those to whom St. Paul wrote the words of our text,

"ALL THE SAINTS SALUTE YOU."

XX.

WELLS AND WATER-PIPES.

"Spring up, O well: Sing ye unto it."
NUMBERS xxi. 17.

A FAR off on the meadows at Narragansett Pier, back by the Point Judith marshes, there used to be a round dell in the rocks, with a bubbling spring in it.

Very few people who go to that seaside place for the summer ever knew about this spring. It used to keep bubbling up amid the tall grass, and only the cows and two or three sojourners there could tell just where to find it. Many a time as I have tramped along over the meadows I have turned aside to get a cup of water from that well among the rocks. Last summer, when I went to the shore, I went to find my dear old well—and lo! it was gone. A house had been built on the field and the well had disappeared. A pipe had taken the place of the well, and the spring was filling a cistern in the house. My dear old well was gone. But it has given me my subject to-day. This sermon is about the difference there is between,

"WELLS AND WATER-PIPES."

Let us study out this subject, and learn the lessons which it teaches us.

The words which I have taken for our text to-day describe the children of Israel when they were journeying through the hot plains of the Desert.

They had left the hill country of the Moabites and the land of the water-brooks, and were now threading their way through the dry sands of the desert. They were tired and weary and faint. It was hot work marching on with their little children and their cattle. The sun was beating down upon them, and it seemed as if they must all die soon of heat and faintness, when suddenly through the long caravan went the cry of "water." They had come to a place where there were indications of hidden springs, and instantly the men in the company went to work and began to dig in the desert. Soon the water burst forth. Men, women and children caught up the cool and sparkling water in bowls and pitchers as it leaped forth in its fountain spray, and the people were saved. And then we read these words, "And from thence they went to Beer:" that is the well whereof the Lord spake unto Moses, "Gather the people together and I will give them water." Then Israel sang this song, "Spring up, O well: sing ye unto it."

This story of the well springing up in the desert reminds us of another story in the Bible, when a greater than Moses sat by a well, and used the well of water as a living picture of that grace of God which sustains our souls with the ever living water of eternal life. The words are taken from the fourth chapter of St. John's gospel, and are as follows:

"Then cometh he to a city of Samaria, which is called Sychar, near to the parcel of ground that Jacob gave to his son Joseph.

"Now Jacob's well was there. Jesus therefore, being wearied with his journey, sat thus on the well: and it was about the sixth hour.

"There cometh a woman of Samaria to draw water: Jesus saith unto her, Give me to drink.

"(For his disciples were gone away unto the city to buy meat.)

"Then saith the woman of Samaria unto him, How is it that thou, being a Jew, askest drink of me, which am a woman of Samaria? for the Jews have no dealings with the Samaritans.

"Jesus answered and said unto her, If thou knewest the gift of God, and who it is that saith to thee, Give me to drink; thou wouldest have asked of him, and he would have given thee living water.

"The woman saith unto him, Sir, thou hast nothing to draw with, and the well is deep: from whence then hast thou that living water?

"Art thou greater than our father Jacob, which gave us the well, and drank thereof himself, and his children, and his cattle?

"Jesus answered and said unto her, Whosoever drinketh of this water shall thirst again:

"But whosoever drinketh of the water that I shall give him shall never thirst; but the water that I shall give him shall be in him a well of water springing up into everlasting life."

I want to speak to you to-day about the two sources of water-supply which we have in life. We shall find that there are the same two sources for our souls.

I.

First of all there is the supply which comes from a water-pipe.

A pipe leads from some well or spring or source of supply, but it is not a source of supply itself. It is made of brick or of tiles, and leads the water from some well or spring into a reservoir or cistern. Sometimes it has a leak in it, and the water escapes. Sometimes it gets filled and choked up with rubbish, and the water will not flow through it. Sometimes it gets full of impurities and gives a foul taste to the water as it passes through it. A drain is very useful, but it is not beautiful. I knew a gentleman who had so many water-pipes on his place at the sea-shore that his wife called the place " Drain Hurst."

Well! my dear children, how much of this drain-pipe business there is with us in life. *We get our supplies from other people.* We draw water from all sorts of sources outside of ourselves. We depend upon such a friend, or such a minister, or such a method of living. We are forever trying to lay pipes from outside sources to get supplies into our life, just as in Philadelphia the water-pipes carry the Schuylkill water from the reservoir at Fairmount to the homes all over the city. If the water in the reservoir is muddy, the water in the houses will be muddy. If the water has a bad odor in the aqueduct, the pipe will carry that same water into our homes. You never can sing to a water-pipe and say, "Spring up, oh, pipe : sing ye unto it." The water-pipe is only a channel from an outside source. It is not a source of supply in itself. There were two women once who went a great deal to church. One seemed to be made better and stronger for going; the other said that going to church did her no good. "What is the reason?" she asked of her friend, "what is the reason that you seem to be made better for going to church, and I keep just where I am all the time?"

"I will tell you," replied her friend. "I go to the services in order to get to Jesus Christ, while you go to the services merely for the sake of going to church." That church was a spring of grace to one woman: it was only an empty channel to the other one!

My dear children, do not depend upon empty channels. Don't get into the way of living by outside sources of supply. They leak; they get filled with rubbish; they become foul. The water-pipe is very well in itself, but there is something much better after all than a pipe that may run dry.

II.

Secondly, there is the supply which comes from the spring. Jesus said to the woman of Samaria, "The water that I shall give him shall be in him a well of water springing up into everlasting life." In another place Jesus said, "The kingdom of God is within you." There is no such source of help and comfort in life as that which comes to us from having our own sources of power within us.

There was a very near-sighted general in the civil war who suddenly found himself face to face with the enemy. In five minutes time he found that he must fight a battle. He sent at once for one of his staff and ordered him to bring his carpet-bag to him. The orderly-sergeant brought the brigadier-general his valise, and the brigadier-general began to get out his books and maps on his saddle pommel, and pulling on his spectacles, tried to find out from the books how he was to fight this battle. In a little while he was told he must scamper off the field as his troops had broken ranks and were flying. He lost that battle because he was trying to get his supply of knowledge through the books, instead of having a well of knowledge springing up within him. My dear children, learn this great lesson of life, that our sources of supply must be within us. Turn your books into brains; turn your outside supplies into internal springs. Learn to know what is right. Learn to know what your duty is. Ask God to open within you the springs of His grace and power. Clear out the weeds, the dirt, the stones and the rubbish, and let the wells of knowledge and duty and motive power spring up within you.

Keep the living springs of love and conscience, of gentleness, of tenderness, of purity and truth, ever open within you.

Thus you will find that when you are moved to do what is brave and true and pure, it is the springs that are within you that are bubbling up in constant motion.

These, then, are the two sources of power which we learn from our subject.

There is the method of the water-pipe, and there is the method of the spring.

The fountain is better than the cistern.

Therefore let us always sing this song:

"Spring up, O well: sing ye unto it."

XXI.

"INNOCENCY."

"Keep innocency and take heed unto the thing that is right, for that shall bring a man peace at the last." —Ps. xxxvii. 38. (From the Psalter Version.)

THERE was once upon a time a king on his way to his capital, which was a long way off, and his road lay through a village. As he went along, the villagers crowded to see him, and stood ranged all along the street. Among them was a young, timid girl, poorly dressed. As the king went by he saw her look sadly and supplicatingly towards him, and he stopped his horse and beckoned her to draw near. She modestly disengaged herself from the throng, and advanced. Then he asked her her name, and whether she was a native of that village, for, in truth she hardly looked like a common country girl. She answered that she was not born there, but was a native of his capital; of that she was by birthright a citizen, but through her parents' fault she had been banished from it, and their great wealth, estates and titles had been forfeited.

"And on what do you live?" asked the king, quite touched.

"I spin for my daily bread," she answered. "I earn enough to clothe and feed myself, and that is all."

"And are you here alone in your exile?" asked the king.

"No sire! I have five brothers."

"But," he further asked, "do they not support you and give you of the fruit of their labor?"

"Sire!" exclaimed the maiden, opening her eyes wide, "they never give me anything, but often beg or borrow of me, and sometimes reduce me to great straits."

"Maiden," said the king, "I will examine into this matter. Here, take this ring, keep it until I return, which will be shortly; I cannot tell you the day, but it will be before long. When I return bring me my ring and I shall remember you by it, and if I have found that your story is true I will reinstate you in all your family honors and wealth. But," he added, with a warning gesture, "if you part with my ring I shall hesitate about trusting you."

Then the king put his ring on her finger and rode away.

Not long after he was gone the news of what had happened came to the ears of the girl's brothers. One of these was a painter, another was a musician, the third a cook, the fourth a gardener, and the fifth was a draper. As soon as the painter could he left his work and hastened to his sister, and looked at the ring. "What a lovely ring!" he exclaimed; "the gold is so fine, and the stone in it sparkles with all kinds of colors. Do, dear sister, lend or give it to me; I want to paint a figure with rings on the fingers, and this will be useful as a pattern. Let me have the ring and I will paint you the most beautiful picture you ever saw; indeed, I will hang pictures all around the room if you will give it to me."

"No, brother," said the girl, "I cannot part with the ring. I have promised to keep it; besides, when I receive my fortune at the king's return, I shall be so rich that I can buy as many pictures as I wish."

The painter then went away dejected, and the musician came next. He also desired the ring. "Look here, sister," he said, "lend me the ring; I am going to a concert, and I want to appear as well dressed and with as many ornaments as I can. Lend it to me just for a bit, and I will give you a ticket for the concert, and you shall hear the most beautiful music for nothing."

"Thank you, brother," said the maid, "I do not know when the king will return, so I must not part with the ring for a moment." So he also went away disappointed. Then came the third brother, the cook, and he also wanted the ring. "My dear sister," he said, "I know how badly you are off, and what poor fare you have. It has always been a trouble to me to think how scanty and mean are your repasts. If you will give me the ring I will send you every day the best dishes I can cook, and the most delicious cakes and sweetmeats in my shop."

"Thank you, brother," answered the damsel, "I fare quite as well as I want. My meals are simple but sufficient, and I had rather wait till I receive my fortune before feasting, than run the risk of losing it by giving up my ring." The next to arrive was the gardener. "My good sister," he said, "come into my garden and let me show you what beautiful flowers I have. How sweet these roses smell, and how fragrant is that wreath of jessamine! Look at that bed of thyme, what a delicious scent it exhales! My sister, if you will give me your ring, I will provide you every day with a bunch of the most perfumed of my flowers."

"I cannot part with the ring," answered the girl, "I have promised to keep it, and I value it above your flowers."

Then came the youngest brother, the draper, and he arrived with a number of boxes. "I have brought you," he said, "some of my most fashionable dresses, for you to see. Did you ever cast your eye on such laces and such silks? And look at the style of the costumes! You will find nothing like them anywhere; and you shall have your pick of them for a trifle."

"Thank you, brother," began the sister, when he interrupted her. "My dear, I am afraid you suffer from the cold in winter; I think you really ought to take more care of your health, and wear furs. Furs are now very fashionable and happen to be extraordinarily cheap. Look here at this beautiful mantle, lined with fur; I want nothing for it but that little ring on your finger. By the way, let me look at it. Gold, do you call it? It is only brass. Do you think that stone a diamond? You are quite mistaken, it is paste. However, as I am your brother, and as I said the word, you shall have the fur cloak. I shall be happy to accommodate you."

"Thank you, dear brother," said the maiden; but she hesitated, for she longed to have the lovely laces and silks even more than the furs. Thank you, brother, I must refuse them; I cannot part with the ring." But she said it with a sigh.

My dear children, this story which I have found in an English book of sermons, is an allegory or parable. The preacher who used the story, says: "The soul is the maiden banished from Heaven, robbed of her high estate and great privileges, by the fault of onr first parents, Adam and Eve. But God has looked on the soul and has promised her restoration. Only, the soul must be tried awhile, and must patiently wait His coming, and, above all, must preserve the ring of Innocence. The soul has five brothers—the senses—sight, hearing, tasting, smelling and feeling; and these are continually assailing her to give up to them her innocency. The soul is ever in danger of forfeiting her innocence through those temptations that come in through the senses. All sorts of pleasures and comforts are robbed by the senses. But in exchange is asked the ring of Innocency."

This sermon to-day is about

"INNOCENCY."

I never read this beautiful psalm as it is found in the psalter for the fourth selection, without thinking of the wonderful calmness which seems to breathe through these words. They form the story and holy experience of the man who wrote them. He was a saint—and these words speak of divine faith and courage.

"Hope thou in the Lord, and keep His way, and He shall promote thee that thou shalt possess the land; when the ungodly shall perish, thou shalt see it. I myself have seen the ungodly in great power, and flourishing like a green bay-tree. I went by, and lo! he was gone. I sought him, but his place could nowhere be found. Keep innocency, and take heed unto the thing that is right: for that shall bring a man peace at the last." * * * *

It is frequently said that life is a game. We sometimes hear people speak of the "game of life." You know how it is with a game. It has its rules, its rewards and its punishments. Take, for instance, the game of "Tivoli." It is a board with tin pegs on it, like pins, and a marble is propelled through this wilderness of pins by a stick with a round end to it. The marble goes on its way through this forest of pins, and then tumbles into certain holes which are marked ten, twenty and fifty *on*, and ten, twenty and fifty *off*.

Well, I have often thought how much the game of Tivoli is like the game of life. We all go out into the stages of life as the marble goes out through the pins, and we fall into holes which are ten "off" our character or twenty "off" our career. What we all want to do is to avoid the holes in life where we get ten off or fifty off of our record. And this brings us to the one question of our subject to-day: "How can I win in the game of life?"

Listen to the answer—it is all found in the words of our text to-day: "Keep innocency and take heed unto the thing which is right, for that shall bring a man peace at the last!"

There are two lessons for us all to learn from our subject to-day.

I.

The first lesson is that Innocency is God's best gift to His Children.

God might have asked us to give Him strength, or beauty, or wisdom, and it might have been very difficult for us to have complied with His commands. But God only asks us to be true and pure and good. He asks us not to conform our lives to the standard of the world about us, but to build up our characters upon the standard of His own divine nature. It is not keeping wisdom or power or beauty: it is keeping innocency, which will bring a man peace at the last. Innocency is the ring which God gives us; and the world, the flesh, and the devil—like the brothers in the story of the maiden and her ring—are trying all they can to rob us of that which God has given us; the one thing within us which is the marriage ring between our souls and God.

In the story of "Pilgrim's Progress," Christian, the hero, is represented as receiving a roll at the wicket-gate from the hands of Evangelist, his guide, which he was told to keep in his bosom until he should cross the river of death, and be received at the gate of the Celestial City.

And, in the same way, my dear children, when we are brought into the Christian Church, we receive a mark or sign which we are to keep as a sacred symbol of purity, until we pass the waves of this troublesome world and come to the land of everlasting life, there to reign with God, world without end.

Dear children—learn to reverence, in your nature, this sacred treasure, this purity or innocency of life. Do not soil your hands, your eyes, your ears, your life with impure thoughts, words and deeds. *Bad words stick.*

Evil thoughts, once lodged in the mind, take root and abide there. Foul expressions, impure stories and low, obscene talk are like the seven devils, which took up their abode in the soul of the man in our Lord's parable, when the man's house was empty, swept and garnished.

Keep innocency: keep innocency in your life, it is God's best gift to His children: it will indeed bring a man peace at the last.

II.

The second lesson of our subject is that Holiness is Man's best gift to God.

Innocency is not holiness: innocency is the stuff out of which holiness is made. Wood and brick and stone and mortar are not the house; they are the materials out of which the house is made. God gives us, in our childhood days, innocency. God wants us in return to give to Him, in our manhood and womanhood, this same innocency turned into holiness.

A ship on the ways when it is launched

from the shipyard is innocent, as it were, of all that is before it. But when it comes back into port again, after a long voyage in which it has conquered the storms and the gales of the ocean, it has added a new element to its work and has won or acquired a character of its own, which is something more than it was when it left the shipyard. A soldier on review in the parade ground is a pretty spectacle with his clean arms and bright uniform. But that same soldier, when he comes back to his friends and his family, after the long, hard campaign, is worth a great deal more than he was when he was a mere holiday soldier.

And in this same way, my dear children, this life which is given to each one of us is only given to us on purpose to know whether or not we will do the will of God. It is like the sea which brings the vessel's power out. It is like the battle which tests and proves the stuff which is in the soldier. Holiness or wickedness is that which we earn for ourselves in life. If we keep innocency it will turn into holiness. If we lose our innocency badness will come up in its place, just as weeds come up in a garden, unless that garden is sown with good seed.

* * * *

Remember then these two lessons of our subject to-day:—

1st. Innocency is God's best gift to His children;—

2d. Holiness is man's best gift to God.

"Keep innocency and take heed unto the thing that is right, for that shall bring a man peace at the last."

* * * *

I want to say one word before I close. I never wrote anything in all my life amid such surroundings as those which have been with me while I have been writing this sermon.

My dear father, so well known to the children of America, and of the world, by his writings, has died since I have written the text of this sermon.

It was my privilege to be with him, day and night, throughout all his sickness. I walked with him until he could walk no more. I wheeled him in a wheeling chair until the day before his death, when he could no longer sit in a chair. I read to him until he could listen no longer, and prayed with him until his consciousness left him. In all my life I never saw such purity and beauty of Christian character, and as the shadows of the grave began to close in upon that strong and holy life, his faith and courage and divine trust in his Saviour stood by him to the last.

It is a solemn thing to die. Everything that is of the earth drops out of our hands then, as the toys do in the hands of tired little children when they fall asleep.

Then we want only the strong and eternal things to keep us, as the things of this life disappear. And so, for myself, I shall never forget these words of our text—as I watched my dear father breathe out his soul in death in the early hours of that bright May morning—" Keep innocency, and take heed to the thing that is right, *for that shall bring a man peace at the last.*"

XXII.

LESSONS FROM THE FERRY-BOAT.

"And there went over a ferry-boat to carry over the King's household."—2 SAM. xix. 18.

THIS sermon is a ferry-boat sermon. A little while ago we had a wheel-barrow sermon. To-day we have as our subject some lessons from the ferry-boat. The way I came to write this sermon was as follows: When coming on to Philadelphia not long ago, while crossing over to Jersey City in one of the Pennsylvania Railroad ferry-boats, I was wondering what I should write about in my next course of children's sermons. All of a sudden it came to me to write about the lessons which we learn from a ferry-boat —and so this ferry-boat sermon came into existence from my ride across the North

River from Courtlandt street to Jersey City.

In the passage where our text is found to-day there is given us a description of the way in which King David came back again to Jerusalem after the death of Absalom. This nineteenth chapter of the first book of Samuel is a very remarkable chapter. First of all came Zadok and Abiathar, the priests, to welcome back the King. Then there came a man named Shimei who had cursed the King when he fled from the city. Now he was very sorry for his treacherous action, and came begging King David to forgive him for his evil conduct. Then there came a son of Saul whose name was Mephibosheth, to explain to the King why it was that he did not go to meet him, since he was lame in his two feet and could not walk. Another man who went to meet the King was named Barzillai. He was a very rich man and lived on the other side of the river Jordan. King David wanted him to cross the river and go and live at Jerusalem, but Barzillai declined, saying, "How long have I to live that I should go up with the King to Jerusalem? I am this day fourscore years old; and can I discern between good and evil? Can thy servant take what I eat or what I drink? Can I hear any more the voice of singing men and singing women? Wherefore, then, should thy servant be yet a burden unto the lord my King? Thy servant will go a little way over Jordan with the King: and why should the King recompense me with such a reward?"

And then we come across the words of our text to-day: "And there went over a ferry-boat to carry over the King's household, and to do what he thought good."

I suppose this "ferry-boat" was a little skiff or scow, such as travellers see to-day on the Highland lochs in Scotland. These skiffs or scows were probably propelled across the water by poles which were pushed down into the bed of the stream in some such way as the lumbermen's rafts up in Maine are pushed by the lumbermen.

Well! I think we can see these people coming down to the river from the opposite side of the banks of the Jordan, to see their dear old King go across the river and return to his capital at Jerusalem. We can see the baggage which they brought down with them to the boat. We can see the cattle which were driven down for the purposes of sacrifice, together with the women and children who wanted to see the last of the King on their side of the river Jordan. In fact it is quite a vivid picture which comes before our eyes when we read these words of our text to-day: "And there went over a ferry-boat to carry over the King's household."

And now let us see what lessons we learn from the ferry-boats. Perhaps you may have crossed over in a modern ferry-boat from New York to Brooklyn, or from Philadelphia to Camden, or from Jersey City to New York, and may have never thought how the ferry-boat can teach us all some very important lessons.

We learn three lessons from the ferry-boats.

I.

First. Ferry-boats are at home on each side of the river.

A ferry-boat is a boat of a very peculiar shape. It is what is called a "double-ender." It has a bow at each end of the boat. There is no difference between the stem and the stern. A ferry-boat will go either way, backward or forward. It never has to turn round. It goes back and forth from slip to slip like a shuttle in a loom. I have watched sparrows on a ferry-boat and they have always seemed to be perfectly at home. Some time ago, on the Jersey City ferry, I watched an old yellow tabby cat with her kittens, who seemed to have her home in the engine-room. I kept wondering whether she paid her taxes in New York or in New Jersey. She seemed to be at home in either place. When a ferry-boat goes into its slip it is at home, no matter on which side of the river it is. The first thing a ferry-boat teaches us is that it is at home on either side of the river.

II.

The second lesson that we learn from a ferry-boat is that ferry-boats *make the connection perfect between opposite shores.* I have often watched a ferry-boat going into its dock. First it bumps on one side; then it bumps on the other side. It rubs up along the side of the slip and lunges along against the piles and makes the passengers totter, but at last it fits into its proper place and comes to a stand still. Then the great hooks are put out into the boat's rings, and the windlass is turned with its crank and chains, and the sound of the ratchet is heard as the clogs in the windlass fall into place. Then the board is put down, the bow chain is dropped, the boat chains are drawn one side, and the passengers and teams cross over the boards and go up the arched way to the street. The ferry-boat has done its work. It has taken the place of a bridge—and is a moving bridge in itself. It has carried the passengers and teams to the other side of the river and has made the connection perfect between the opposite shores.

III.

The third lesson we learn from the ferry-boat is that *ferry-boats are guided by a directing eye.* There is always in every ferry-boat a man at the wheel in the wheel-house. Passengers go on board; horses and wagons loaded with freight wait patiently until the boat crosses; the boat moves on amid ice and rain and fog, and carefully finds its way across the harbor, crowded as it is with boats of steam and sail. Small boats get in the way; ocean steamers cross the path; the ferry-boat steams and stops and whistles; the engines obey the sound of the bell from the wheel-house, and in this way this moving world of life is safely landed by the skill and power of the all-seeing eye at the wheel. "I will guide thee with my eye" is a text which might well adorn every wheel-house in its high and lofty perch.

These, then, are the three lessons which we learn from the ferry-boat.

Ferry-boats are at home on each side of the river; ferry-boats make the connection perfect between opposite shores; ferry-boats are guided by an all-directing eye.

Now then, my dear children, let us apply these lessons to our subject to-day.

What the ferry-boat is to the passengers who use it, *God's revelation of truth is to the soul of man.* God has provided a means of communication between Himself and us. This revelation of His truth is like the ferry-boat for our souls. The Gospel of the Lord Jesus Christ, as given us in the Bible and in the Christian Church, is the divinely appointed means by which we can get from this world to Him, from this side of the river of death to the bright shore of Heaven.

First of all—like the ferry-boat—this gospel of the Lord Jesus Christ is at home on each side of the river of death. It comes to

LESSONS FROM THE FERRY-BOAT. 317

us here in all our sin and darkness and temptation, and fits into our wants, just as the ferry-boat fits into its slip. The gospel fits right into all our human needs. It is not a philosophy only for the rich and the powerful and the great. It is something which comes into the life of us all and fits our needs, so that we can step right upon its broad platform and can trust ourselves to that power which will carry us safely across the waves of this troublesome life to God. It fits into the life that is to be, and yet at the same time it fits into the life which now is.

Secondly, like the ferry-boat, this gospel of the Lord Jesus makes the connection perfect between opposite shores. Jesus said unto his disciples: "My sheep shall never perish, neither shall any man pluck them out of my hands."

It is a great comfort to us when we start out on a long voyage or a long land journey, to feel that we will be brought safely through to our journey's end. It is a great comfort to feel that those who have the charge of the ship or the train know what they are about, and are able to fulfil the contract and bring us safely through. And this is what St. Paul had in mind when he said of our Lord, "He is able to keep that which I have committed to Him against that day." When we feel our own weakness, feebleness and sin, when it seems to us as if we never should be able to overcome the temptations which are about us and get safely through at the last, then there is no such comfort in all the world like that which comes to us when we feel that the Lord Jesus Christ has carried other people through, and will do the same for us if we only are true and faithful to Him.

Thirdly—like the ferry-boat—the gospel of the Lord Jesus Christ is guided by an All-Seeing Eye.

God knows just how much we can stand. God knows just what trials and difficulties are in our way. We cannot see all the way through life. We cannot see the hidden difficulties in our way. But God sees the end from the beginning. His eye looks far across the hidden way of our life. God's hand is upon the machinery of our life. He moves us forward. He bids us stop. He saves us from this difficulty and from that obstacle. Through all the fog and cloud and storm, amid other jarring lives which at any moment might come into collision with us and ruin us—His eye and His hand protect us, and His all-wise Providence directs our way, just as the man at the wheel guides the boat across the crowded harbor. These, then, are the lessons which we learn from the ferry-boat. Let us thank God that there goes over a ferry-boat to carry over the King's household, and let us see to it, my dear young friends, that we have a place among that household—that we, too, may safely be carried through life until we reach that happy shore where we shall see the King in His beauty.

XXIII.

"SPIRITS IN PRISON."

"He went and preached unto the spirits in prison."
1 Pet. iii. 19.

SOME time ago I was up at a boat-house on a certain lake among the Berkshire Hills. While we were waiting for the horses to be harnessed which were to take us home, the owner of the boat-house showed us some animals which he had trapped in the woods. There were three or four red foxes in a box, a hedgehog, a muskrat and some wild birds. Among the birds was a fine young eagle, with broad wings and a splendid white head. I admired the eagle very much, but I pitied the poor bird with all my heart. *An American eagle was a prisoner in a parrot's cage.*

I want to speak to you to-day about "Spirits

in prison." That eagle in a parrot's cage was a symbol of what is meant by a spirit in prison. He was never meant to be kept in a parrot's cage. He was a captive. He was in wrong surroundings. It was a gilded cage—but still it was a cage. He was a spirit in prison.

What St. Peter means by this verse it is very hard to understand. He is speaking of the way in which our Lord entered the world of spirits after His death upon the cross. When His body was laid in the tomb of Joseph of Arimathea, the spirit of Jesus, with the soul of the penitent thief, entered into Paradise. There, in a world of spirits, were many souls who had never heard of Jesus. They were spirits shut up, as it were, in prison. To *these* spirits Jesus preached, and told them of the deliverance of the world by His mission of Salvation into it.

Perhaps the words may have another meaning—but this is enough for our subject to-day. They tell us this much at least, that Jesus Christ our Lord and Master tried to let the spirits free who had never heard of Him, and who were in prison in the dark world of the lost.

Our sermon to-day is about

"SPIRITS IN PRISON."

We are not all body. We are not all mind. We are not all spirit. The body comes first, and is like the foundation of the house: the mind comes next and is like the middle stones of the house: the spirit comes last and is like the roof or dome of the building. We have each of us a spirit imprisoned or caged in our body. And that spirit in the cage or prison of the body is waiting to be set free either by the power of God or by the power of Satan. God holds the key of the soul's prison in His hand; but Satan also has a false key to the heart of man. He is a thief and a robber, and is the father of lies. He too wants to get hold of these spirits in prison and set them free for his own service.

We learn three lessons to-day from this sermon about the Spirits in prison.

I.

First of all we learn that there is a hidden spirit in every one of us.

When we go into the country in the winter time everything in nature seems to be dead. The trees are dead, and are without leaves; the little brooks and lakes are frozen over; the sound of the rippling brooks is not heard, and all the plants and flowers are covered over with a mantle of snow. There is a verse which St. Paul cites in this sense, when he says of some of his converts: "Ye are dead, and your life is hid with Christ in God." He means by this that these converts of his had a life which was hidden from the world, a life which the world could not see.

Now, then, each one of us has a hidden life, or a hidden spirit, which those about us do not see. It takes us a long time to find out just what we really are. Perhaps it is some duty or trial, or great responsibility which brings the hidden spirit out. In this way it very often happens that our trials are blessings in disguise. When the little eaglets are taken out from their nests by the mother eagle, they are carried on her back for awhile, and then the mother bird tosses them off and lets them fly for themselves. No doubt the young eagles think this is severe treatment on the part of their mother, but then it is just this which makes them strong and gives them their power of wing. And this is what Moses had in view when he said of the children of Israel, "As an eagle stirreth up her nest, fluttereth over her young, spreadeth abroad her wings, taketh them, beareth them on her wings—so the Lord alone did lead him, and there was no strange God with him." Just as there is a hidden life in the trees and brooks and plants in the winter time, so there is a hidden spirit or life in each one of us. What we are is not all seen at once, and upon the surface. There is a hidden life or spirit in us all which is under the surface, just as the brook flows on under the snow ; just as the sap of the tree flows on beneath the trunk. This hidden spirit may be imprisoned in our body; it may be handcuffed or fettered to some sin or temptation; it may be bound to a gang of evil habits as the convicts are bound together by a chain around their legs, but there it is in us all the while. It is something which is hidden or imprisoned in us all.

II.

Secondly, we learn that the hidden spirit in us needs bringing out. Perhaps we may wonder in the winter time how it can be possible for the ice and snow to disappear, and how the trees and plants and flowers can ever bud and blossom again. They do not spring into new life of themselves. It is the sun in the heavens which sets the imprisoned life in nature free. The sun shines and the crops appear; the sun shines and the brooks begin to ripple again; the sun shines and the flowers come to life; the sun shines and the singing birds which have been hidden all come forth to the light. The sun in the heavens is a great preacher, a very drawing preacher to all vegetable life upon the earth. The sun preaches to the spirits in nature and brings all their hidden power out.

Here is a violin. I cannot play it; I cannot bring out the hidden music which is there. But presently some skilled performer takes it in his hand, and placing before him the music of Beethoven, or some great master, reproduces that music on the strings of the instrument. The music is already there in the violin. It has only needed bringing out. The music which has been imprisoned there needs to be preached to until it comes forth.

When Michael Angelo, the great sculptor, was working at his statue of Moses, he was so enthusiastic over his work, that, upon one occasion, he failed to take notice that Pope Julius and his cardinals had entered his studio and were standing by his side: "Don't stop me," "don't stop me," he said at last, when he saw them in his studio. "I am trying to get Moses out of this marble: he is imprisoned there."

Well, my dear children, the hidden spirit which is in us all needs bringing out, just as the hidden life in nature needs to be brought out by the sun; or the music in the violin needs to be brought out by the musician, or the image in the marble needs to be hewed out by the sculptor. We do not know how true and strong and good we can become until the spirit which is imprisoned in the cage of our body is preached to or worked upon by the spirit of God. God is to our hidden spirit what the sun is to the crops, or the musician is to the violin, or the sculptor is to the marble.

And this brings us to our last lesson.

III.

Thirdly, we learn that God alone can set the imprisoned spirit free.

A very strange book has been written in the year past about a man who had the power of being a good man and a bad man, just as he chose. When he became a good man he was known as Dr. Jekyll; when he became a bad man he was known as Mr. Hyde. When Mr. Hyde could not be found, Dr. Jekyll was seen, when Dr. Jekyll could not be found, Mr. Hyde was seen on the streets.

At last this strange power of turning from the good man to the bad man was lost, and, having become the bad Mr. Hyde, he never could change back again to the good Dr. Jekyll. His power to be good was gone, like a magnetic battery which has lost its power.

Well, my dear children, of course this is only a story, a fable, and yet there is a great deal of truth in it. The angel and the demon are in us all alike. If the spirit which is in us is not set free in the path of righteousness, it will be let loose some day in the path of wickedness.

This spirit which is imprisoned within us, like the eagle in the parrot's cage, will turn our life to God or to Satan according to the way in which it is set free.

At the battle of Waterloo both Napoleon, on the side of the French, and Wellington, on the side of the English, were expecting reinforcements.

Grouchey, was the name of the marshal who was looked for impatiently by Napoleon. Blucher, was the name of the Prussian General, whom the Duke of Wellington was expecting. Grouchey failed to arrive; Blucher came upon the field early in the afternoon. The coming of Blucher turned the tide of victory upon the side of Wellington, and Napoleon was defeated.

And in this same way, my dear children, the spirit which is within us, when once it is set free, will turn our lives towards sin or towards God. God and God's power alone added to our lives, can turn the fact of life into victory and can make a success of our living. "If God be for us who can be against us?"

Now, then, in closing, my dear children, I beg you to remember that the angel and the demon are in us all alike. If the demon in us is set free and is let loose from the cage or prison where it is confined, it will carry us to destruction. If the angel spirit in us is let loose from the prison-house of the body, it will bring us safely, over all sin and temptation, to God.

Therefore let the Gospel of the Lord Jesus Christ preach to your spirits, now and here in time, in the cage of the body, with all its sins and infirmities, and you will be delivered here in this world from the bondage of corruption into the glorious liberty of the children of God.

XXIV.

"THE LION AND THE BEAR."

"Thy servant slew both the lion and the bear."
1 SAM. xvii. 36.

WE all like to go and see a menagerie. There is something about animals which is very attractive to us. Perhaps it is because we feel that in a certain way we are one with them. Perhaps it is because we see in the animals certain traits which we see and feel to be in ourselves, and in this we cannot help feeling that in some way they are our relations. When I was a boy, in Philadelphia, there was a menagerie at Walnut and Eighth streets, where we used to go on Saturday afternoons. We were allowed to climb up the back of an elephant by a ladder, and then ride round a sawdust ring on the elephant's back, as we sat in a little palanquin—while the keeper sat on his neck and punched him on the head with a stick. Then there was a man who entered a box filled with royal Bengal tigers and leopards, and performed with them, to the great delight of the children. Menageries and panoramas have given place in these days to circuses and cycloramas; but somehow it seems to me that the old Saturday afternoon amusements were better.

Our sermon to-day is a sort of menagerie sermon, and is about

"THE LION AND THE BEAR."

Now these words of our text are found in David's answer to king Saul, when the king wanted him to put on his armor and fight Goliath with it. David did not want to fight the Philistine Giant in Saul's armor, and preferred to take the shepherd's sling with the pebbles from the brook. In giving an account of his life to the king, he told of his exploits as a shepherd boy, and used these words of our text to-day.

"And David said unto Saul, thy servant kept his father's sheep, and there came a lion and a bear and took a lamb out of the flock; and I went out after him, and smote him, and delivered it out of his mouth; and when he arose against me, I caught him by his beard and slew him. Thy servant slew both the lion and the bear, and this Philistine shall be as one of them, seeing he hath defied the armies of the living God. David said moreover, the Lord that delivered me out of the paw of the lion, and out of the paw of the bear, He will deliver me out of the hand of the Philistine. And Saul said unto David—go, and the Lord be with thee."

David was a great fighter all his life. He began his life by fighting animals. He continued by fighting himself; he ended his life by fighting others.

These were the three kinds of enemies he always had, and upon these he exerted all his strength. He began by fighting beasts.

He continued by fighting himself ; he ended by fighting the enemies of the Lord.

*　　　*　　　*　　　*

My dear children, this ought to be the order for each one of us in the matter of fighting sin. We ought to begin by fighting the beast, as David did, and we ought to begin by fighting the beast element which is in us all.

*　　　*　　　*　　　*

I want to speak to you to-day about fighting two beasts which are caged within us all, just as the wild beasts are caged at the menagerie. We have, each one of us, a moral menagerie within us, and, sometimes the wild beasts that are in us get headway and need the whip and the lash of the keeper and the trainer to keep them in order.

"Thy servant slew both the lion and the bear."

I.

First of all we must fight the lion in our nature. The lion is said to be the king of beasts, but he is a fierce kind of king, "As fierce as a lion" has come to be a proverb. When Daniel was thrown into the den of lions it was supposed, by the nobles who had him thrown there, that they were putting him in as bad a place as it was possible for them to find. Those nobles supposed that Daniel would not have ten minutes' worth of life left in him from the first moment when he touched the den.

In Dr. Livingstone's book of travels in Africa, he describes the way in which on one occasion he was seized by a lion in a jungle. The great hairy beast broke his shoulder blade with his paw, and was just about to take a piece out of him when Dr. Livingstone's guide shot him. The doctor says in his book that he never had such a scene of terror and fright as when that African lion in the jungle laid his paw upon him and looked down upon his upturned face as he lay in the tall marsh grass. Now this lion trait of fierceness and cruelty is in us all. We are animals by nature. We have fiery passions and fierce anger. We have hatred, and malice, and envy, and evil-speaking within us. We love to have our own way and to show our teeth and our claws, and our own evil and imperious will.

There was a little boy once who used to give way to his anger by storming out in the nursery at his little sister. Whenever he would get these angry spells on him and roar out at his sister, the nurse would say: "*Hear the lion roar.*" Then she used to make a noise like a lion, and this would make them all laugh, and then they would become good-natured again.

"Thy servant slew both the lion and the bear." Begin the fight of life, my dear children, by fighting the beast nature that is within you. Begin at the very beginning. Fight the lion which is in you—the habit of anger and wrath and fierceness.

II.

But David fought another beast in his own nature. "Thy servant slew both the lion and the bear.

We must fight the bear nature within us.

Bears are very curious animals. We can learn a great many lessons from the ways and habits of bears.

Up in Pittsfield, where I live, every spring of the year there come into the streets of the town two Canadians with a dancing bear. They travel down from Canada through Vermont, and exhibit their bear all through the Berkshire Valley. One of the men blows a bugle, and the other man leads the bear and his dancing pole. When they sit down to lunch they all lunch together, and drink beer together, and lie over on the grass together. The men have not taken the bear out of the forest and made a man of him. On the contrary, the bear has taken the manhood out of the men, and has made them both as bearish as he is. In fact, as you see them walking up the street together, you would think that three bears had come to town and were seeing the sights.

Now the "bear" is in us all. We can all be "bearish" if we want to be so, if we only let the bear element in us get headway.

It is said that the mother bear licks her cubs into shape when they are little, and in this way makes them presentable to the rest of their relations.

After the mother bear has spent all her skill and energy in this way the young bears are supposed to be educated, and to be fitted for the duties and responsibilities of bear society. I was reading the other day a fable about this habit among the bears. It appears a mother bear was very much afraid that a great lion, who lived in the forest near them, might some day devour her young ones when they were off at play, or had gone on errands; so she told her fears to the lion one day when he was paying the bear family a social call. The lion in a very polite way declared that nothing would be further from his intentions than to hurt her children, if he could only tell how he was to know her cubs.

"O," replied the mother bear, "nothing can be easier. You will know my little dears at once; they are the most beautiful cubs in the world; their education is all finished; I have just finished licking them into shape."

The lion bade the family adieu, and set off on his journey home through the forest. Feeling very faint and hungry, he was at a loss to know how he was to find any refreshment, when all of a sudden he came upon two fat little cubs waddling home. After a few short struggles he fell upon the cubs and made a good meal out of them, and then pursued his way home. The next day he was called upon by the stricken mother, who expressed her surprise at his unfeeling action, whereupon he replied, "My dear madam, nothing can give me greater pain than to think of the unfortunate mistake which has been made; but I really found it quite impossible to see in the ugly little cubs which I devoured, the beautiful creatures which you so eloquently described to me."

Now, my dear children, there is no mistaking the fact that many boys are little else than young bears who need to be trained into shape. This is what school does for us; this is what our true friends do for us; this is what society does for us. All education—and all Christian education, is intended to get the bear out of us and to mould us into fitting shape. Learn then not to be bearish. Learn to fight the bear in you—and to keep it down under your firm and strong Christian will.

In the city of Berne, in Switzerland, there is a monument in the market place to the Burgundian Duke, who, many hundred years ago, founded that city. He killed a bear on that spot, and when he founded the city he named it Berne—the Burgundian word for bear. As I looked at the statue, one day, in the market place, I found that there was a motto on it, which motto I put in my note book. That motto is as follows: "*E Bellua cœsa sit nomen urbis*"—"From a bear slain let the city take its name." And so I say to you to-day—From the bear slain in your nature let the name of your true character be made. Kill the bear in you and build up a new character on the spot where the bear was slain.

The Lion and the Bear.

"Thy servant slew both the lion and the bear."

Now then, my dear children, begin the fight of life with David by fighting the animal in your own nature. Fight being fierce and cross; fight being bearish and sullen. Get the beast nature out of your life and character, and when you have fought the beasts that are in you, God will give you strength to fight the giants which are around you—as he gave David the strength to fight Goliath—by giving him, first of all, the strength in the days of his young shepherd life to fight the lion and the bear. Ask the Lord Jesus Christ to help you; for He came into this world on purpose to give us strength and power to overthrow the works of the devil.

Being fierce and being sullen are the two animals in our nature we all have to fight in life.

Ask the Lord Jesus Christ to give you power to overcome both of these; so that like David you may "slay both the lion and the bear."

MARCH, 1887

BOOKS

PUBLISHED BY

ROBERT CARTER & BROTHERS,

530 BROADWAY, NEW YORK.

THE CRISIS OF MISSIONS; or, The Voice out of the Cloud. By the Rev. ARTHUR T. PIERSON, D.D. 16mo $1.25

"It is as fascinating as a novel, and yet overflowing with facts that make one wonder how it can be possible that such great progress has been made in missions, even during the recent years, and he not have known more of it. This book can but stimulate the followers of Christ to greater love for, and more earnest efforts in, missions." — *Christian Work.*

"This is a book for every Christian to read with prayer and a sincere desire to know his personal duty in this great and glorious work." — *New York Observer.*

"In the little volume before us, the history of missions is unrolled as a scroll, the marvellous providences of God are traced in letters which glow with the intensity of the writer's convictions, the trumpet-call of God's providences to the Christian world is sounded so loud and clear as to reach, one would think, the dullest ear." — *Baptist Herald.*

"One of the most important books to the cause of Foreign Missions — and through them to Home Missions also — which ever has been written. It should be in every library and every household. It should be read, studied, taken to heart, and prayed over." — *Congregationalist.*

*A. L. O. E. LIBRARY.

50 vols., 16mo, in a neat wooden case, *net* 28.00

"All these stories have the charm and pure Christian character which have made the name of A. L. O. E. dear to thousands of homes." — *Lutheran.*

ARNOT, Rev. William.

On the Parables. 12mo 1.75
Church in the House; or, Lessons on the Acts of the Apostles. 12mo 1.50

BERNARD, T. D.
    The Progress of Doctrine in the New Testament. 12mo $1.25
    "The style is absolutely perfect. A broad, deep stream of fresh thought, in language as clear as crystal, flows through the whole devout, instructive, quickening, and inspiring work. Simply as a model of style, every preacher might profitably study it.... This volume makes the New Testament a new book to me." — *Rev. T. L. Cuyler, D.D.*

BICKERSTETH, Rev. E. H.
    Yesterday, To-day, and Forever. A Poem. Pocket edition, $0.50; 16mo, $1.00; 12mo 1.50
    "If any poem is destined to endure in the companionship of Milton's hitherto matchless epic, we believe it will be 'Yesterday, To-day, and Forever.'" — *London Globe.*

BLUNT'S Coincidences and Paley's Horæ Paulinæ. 12mo 1.50

BONAR, Horatius, D.D.
    Hymns of Faith and Hope. 3 vols. 16mo 2.25
    Bible Thoughts and Themes. 6 vols. 12mo 12.00
    Way of Peace 0.50
    Way of Holiness 0.60
    Night of Weeping 0.50
    Morning of Joy 0.60
    Follow the Lamb 0.40
    How shall I go to God? 0.40

BOWES, Rev. G. S.
    Scripture its own Illustrator. 12mo 1.50
    Information and Illustration. 12mo 1.50

BRODIE, Emily.
    Jean Lindsay, The Vicar's Daughter 1.25
    Dora Hamilton's Choice. 12mo 1.25
    Elsie Gordon. 12mo 1.25
    Uncle Fred's Shilling. 12mo 1.25
    Lonely Jack. 12mo 1.25
    Ruth's Rescue. 16mo 0.50
    Nora Clinton. 12mo 1.25
    The Sea Gull's Nest. 16mo 0.60
    Norman and Elsie. 12mo 1.25
    Five Minutes too Late 1.25
    East and West 0.60
    His Guardian Angel 1.25

CHARLESWORTH, Miss M. L.
    Ministering Children. 12mo 1.50
        "   " 16mo 1.00
    Sequel to Ministering Children. 12mo 1.50
        "   "   " 16mo 1.00

CHARLESWORTH, Miss M. L., *continued.*
   Oliver of the Mill. 12mo $1.00
   Dorothy Cope, containing "The Old Looking-Glass" and
   "Broken Looking-Glass." 12mo 1.50

CUYLER, Rev. T. L.
   Pointed Papers. 12mo 1.50
   Thought Hives. 12mo 1.50
   From Nile to Norway 1.50
   Empty Crib. 24mo 1.00
   Cedar Christian. 18mo 0.75
   Stray Arrows. 18mo 0.60
   God's Light on Dark Clouds. Flexible, red edges . . . 0.75

"In this beautiful little volume the author presents a grateful offering to the 'desponding and bereaved.' . . . He offers to others what he has tested for himself. The book is written out of a full heart and a vivid experience." — *Presbyterian Review.*

*D'AUBIGNÉ, Dr. Merle.
   *History of the Reformation in the Sixteenth Century.
   5 vols., 12mo, cloth, in a box 4.50
   *History of the Reformation in the Time of Calvin. 8 vols.,
   12mo, cloth, in a box 8.00

"The work is now complete; and these later volumes, together with the original five, form a library relating to the Reformation of incalculable value and of intense interest. The pen of this master of history gave a charm to everything that he touched." — *New York Observer.*

   *A very cheap edition of Reformation in the Sixteenth
   Century. 5 vols. in one, 890 pages, cloth 1.00

DICKSON, Rev. Alexander, D.D.
   All about Jesus. 12mo 2.00
   Beauty for Ashes. 12mo 2.00

"His book is a 'bundle of myrrh,' and will be specially enjoyed by those who are in trouble." — *Rev. Dr. W. M. Taylor.*

"Luscious as a honeycomb, with sweetness drawn from God's Word." — *Rev. Dr. Cuyler.*

DRINKWATER, Jennie M.
   Only Ned. 12mo 1.25
   Not Bread Alone. 12mo 1.25
   Fred and Jeanie. 12mo 1.25
   Tessa Wadsworth's Discipline. 12mo 1.50
   Rue's Helps. 12mo 1.50
   Electa; A Story. 12mo 1.50
   Fifteen. 12mo 1.50
   Bek's First Corner. 12mo 1.50
   Miss Prudence. 12mo 1.50
   The Story of Hannah. 12mo 1.50
   That Quisset House 1.50
   Isobel's Between-Times 1.50

EDWARDS, Jonathan.
  *Works. In 4 vols. 8vo $6.00

"I consider Jonathan Edwards the greatest of the sons of men." — *Robert Hall.*

FRASER, Dr. D.
  Synoptical Lectures on the Books of Holy Scripture. New and revised edition. 2 vols. 12mo 4.50

"The plan is to give a general view of the scope and contents of each book in the Bible. It is designed not for professional students alone, but for all educated Christians. The careful reader will gain from, its pages clear ideas of the arrangement, subject-matter, and salient features of the Sacred Scriptures." — *New York Observer.*

GIBERNE, Agnes.
  Aimée. A Tale of James II. 12mo 1.50
  The Curate's Home. 16mo 1.25
  Floss Silverthorn. 16mo 1.25
  Coulyng Castle. 16mo 1.50
  Muriel Bertram. 12mo 1.50
  The Sun, Moon, and Stars. 12mo 1.50
  The World's Foundations; or, Geology for Beginners. 12mo 1.50
  Through the Linn. 16mo 1.25
  Sweetbriar. 12mo 1.50
  Duties and Duties. 16mo 1.25
  Jacob Witherby. 16mo 0.60
  Decima's Promise. 12mo 1.25
  Twilight Talks. 16mo 0.75
  Kathleen. 12mo 1.50
  Daily Evening Rest. 18mo 1.00
  Beryl and Pearl. 12mo 1.50
  Old Umbrellas. 12mo 0.90
  Among the Stars; or, Wonders in the Sky. 12mo . . . 1.50
  Madge Hardwicke 1.00
  Father Aldur: a Water Story 1.50

GREEN, Prof. Wm. Henry, D.D.
  The Argument of the Book of Job Unfolded. 12mo . . 1.75

"That ancient composition, so marvellous in beauty and so rich in philosophy, is here treated in a thoroughly analytical manner, and new depths and grander proportions of the divine original portrayed. It is a book to stimulate research." — *Methodist Recorder.*

  Moses and the Prophets. 12mo, cloth 1.00

"It has impressed me as one of the most thorough and conclusive pieces of apologetics that has been composed for a long time. The critic confines himself to the positions laid down by Smith, and, without being diverted by any side issues or bringing in any other views of other theorists, replies to those positions in a style that carries conviction." — *Professor W. G. T. Shedd, D.D.*

  The Hebrew Feasts. 12mo 1.50

www.ingramcontent.com/pod-product-compliance
Lightning Source LLC
Chambersburg PA
CBHW032355230426
43672CB00007B/707